the small business
handbook

PEARSON
Prentice Hall
BUSINESS

Books that make you better

Books that make you better. That make you *be* better, *do* better, *feel* better. Whether you want to upgrade your personal skills or change your job, whether you want to improve your managerial style, become a more powerful communicator, or be stimulated and inspired as you work.

Prentice Hall Business is leading the field with a new breed of skills, careers and development books. Books that are a cut above the mainstream – in topic, content and delivery – with an edge and verve that will make you better, with less effort.

Books that are as sharp and smart as you are.

Prentice Hall Business.
We work harder – so you don't have to.

For more details on products, and to contact us, visit
www.pearsoned.co.uk

Steve Parks

the small business handbook

The Complete Guide to Running and Growing Your Business

Harlow, England • London • New York • Boston • San Francisco • Toronto
Sydney • Tokyo • Singapore • Hong Kong • Seoul • Taipei • New Delhi
Cape Town • Madrid • Mexico City • Amsterdam • Munich • Paris • Milan

PEARSON EDUCATION LIMITED

Edinburgh Gate
Harlow CM20 2JE
Tel: +44 (0)1279 623623
Fax: +44 (0)1279 431059
Website: www.pearsoned.co.uk

First published in Great Britain in 2006

ISBN-13: 978-0-273-69531-8
ISBN-10: 0-273-69531-2

British Library Cataloguing-in-Publication Data
A catalogue record for this book is available from the British Library

Library of Congress Cataloging-in-Publication Data
A catalog record for this book is available from the Library of Congress

10 9 8 7 6 5 4 3 2
10 09 08 07 06 05

Typeset in 11pt Minion by 70
Printed and bound in Great Britain by Henry Ling Ltd., Dorchester

The publisher's policy is to use paper manufactured from sustainable forests.

For Serge Massicotte, a great entrepreneur
in the making.

Contents

CD contents

Audio – put the disc into a normal CD player to hear:

Track 1: Advice on Sales and Customers

Track 2: Interview with Sahar Hashemi, founder of Coffee Republic

Track 3: Advice on Employing People

Track 4: Interview with Richard Reed, founder of Innocent Drinks

Track 5: Advice on Managing the Money

Track 6: Interview with Liz Jackson, founder of Great Guns Marketing

Track 7: Advice on Running the Business

Track 8: Interview with Simon Woodroffe, founder of Yo! Sushi and star of BBC TV's *Dragons' Den*.

Data – put the disc into your computer to access:

A range of useful forms, templates and tools that you can adapt and use in your own business, including:

● Template invoices

● Template employment contract

● Template cash flow forecast

● And much more

About this book

This book is intended to be a useful, easily understood guide to running and growing a business: the detail 'stuff' that all entrepreneurs have to work through in order to build a successful company.

I hope it will be interesting, but above all else I hope it will be invaluable to have by your desk as you grow your business.

It contains a lot of things I have learned the hard way, and my hope is that my experiences can enable you to tread an easier path as a result. But any entrepreneur has challenges to face and my main piece of advice is 'never, ever give up'.

START-UPS

If you are in the process of starting your own business then this book is best used in conjunction with my book *Start Your Business Week by Week*, also published by Prentice Hall Business. It does exactly what the title suggests and gives you a clearly laid out approach to what you need to do each week for six months to begin your new venture.

WEBSITE

There is a website to support this book at **www.flyingstartups.com/ handbook**. FlyingStartups is an online community for people who are starting and growing their own business. You can read material that supports this book and network with other people who are dealing with similar issues in their businesses.

At the site we call entrepreneurs 'Pilots' to go with the flying theme, and you can keep your own Pilot's Log – a diary (or blog) of the growth of your business, recording the highs and lows for you to look back on in years to come and for others to learn from too.

You'll find that if you do keep a Pilot's Log people will give you lots of feedback, ideas and contacts. Take a look at some of the Logs already on the site to see what I mean.

I'll also be holding occasional live chats online if there are any questions you'd like to ask.

ADDED VALUE CD

Inside the back cover of this book you will find a compact disc. It's cleverly designed to be dual purpose:

Audio CD

If you put the CD into any normal audio CD player you'll be able to listen to interviews with four top entrepreneurs:

- Simon Woodroffe, the founder of Yo! Sushi and star of BBC TV's *Dragons' Den*.

- Sahar Hashemi, founder of Coffee Republic and author of a best-selling book for start-up entrepreneurs, *Anyone Can Do It*.

- Richard Reed, co-founder of Innocent Drinks, a company that makes fruit smoothies.

- Liz Jackson, a young entrepreneur who has built a £2m business called Great Guns Marketing and has won many awards for her work along the way.

You'll hear each of these entrepreneurs give advice on the four main subjects of this book: Sales and Customers, Employing People, Managing the Money and Running the Business.

You'll also hear a full interview with each entrepreneur about their own story and their experiences.

Data CD

If you put the same CD into your computer you'll find that it contains a whole host of supporting documents to go with this book. This includes:

- Sample documents such as meeting agenda, invoices, etc.

- Template documents ready for you to adapt for your company and use, including template legal contracts provided by **www.simply-docs.co.uk**, along with a special offer on website membership, giving you access to a complete range of template contracts.

This CD is given as a free bonus to this book and unfortunately we cannot provide any warranties or technical support.

UPDATES

The regulations, legislation, taxes and other details that this book refers to will, by their very nature, change from time to time.

You can find a regularly updated list of key changes online at **www.flyingstartups.com/updates**.

Acknowledgements

My first thanks must go to my publisher Rachael Stock. Not only for being so helpful and supportive, but also for believing in me enough to commission this title even before my first book had reached the shops!

Next I want to thank everyone else at Prentice Hall Business who has helped bring this book from my brain into your hands, including: Julie Knight, Benjamin Roberts, Cat Timothy, Lucy Blackmore, Graham Henry and his team, Simon Pollard and his team, and the boss-man Richard Stagg.

I'd also like to say hello and thank you to all the members of the FlyingStartups web community whose fascinating and inspiring Pilot's Logs, and willingness to help each other build businesses, have spurred me on to write more books.

As ever, my colleagues at The Red Group have been really supportive, and their expertise and hard work has allowed me the time away from the office to write this, especially Pam Reed, Debbie Saunders and Geoff Windas. Many thanks to them, and to the investors who back our adventures.

Thanks to my family: Roger, Sarah and Jenny Parks. Finally, many thanks to my ever patient girlfriend Anna.

Introduction

What is an entrepreneur? My definition is a simple one: 'A business owner with ambition'.

An entrepreneur's ambition is what takes them a step or more beyond what everybody else achieves. Entrepreneurs create jobs, giving people challenging and rewarding work with a mission. Entrepreneurs create wealth for themselves and the nation by constantly attracting new customers and creating new sales – not just coasting when they've paid the rent for the month. Entrepreneurs create innovation by applying their mind to problems people have missed or dismissed.

Entrepreneurs change the world.

But obviously, we entrepreneurs are expected to know how to do this from birth: absorbing knowledge about recruiting and motivating people from inside the womb, working out cash flow forecasting in the cot and mastering credit control in nursery school.

As so many entrepreneurs now know: you start with an idea, you go for it, you open the business, and then? Then you realize you have to work out a better way to find customers and make sales, develop a system to manage the money, learn how to recruit, motivate and manage staff, and cope with all the rules and regulations.

Our education simply does not prepare us for *any* of the issues we face.

As a result, so many entrepreneurs struggle with so many of the fundamental issues of running their business. I know, because I learned pretty much everything in this book the hard way!

Within this book we'll focus on the key things you need to know to run your business smoothly and successfully, meaning that the admin and management of the company can take up less of your time – allowing you to focus on winning new sales and managing your team.

I hope this book will take some of the weight off your mind, prevent you from learning some things the hard way and help you focus on what is fun in your business, knowing that all the other stuff is taken care of.

WHAT WE'LL COVER

There's a lot to go through, but some of the main headaches we'll solve for you are:

1. What rules and regulations you need to comply with, and how to do that.

2. How to find, recruit, motivate, retain and manage good staff.

3. How to find, attract and sell to new customers.

4. How to raise proper funding for your business.

5. How to ensure you don't run out of cash.

6. How to make sure customers pay on time.

7. How to run better management meetings.

8. How to get your business online – cheaply!

9. How to deal with the most common problems faced by entrepreneurs

10. And much, much more.

There will be useful tools and handy tips along the way – and many of the documents I refer to can be found on the CD-Rom in template form for you to adapt as you wish for use in your business.

But don't forget to have fun. Not many people get to realize their dreams in the way that you are able to. Make the most of it, and when you attain one dream, start aiming for another.

Remember, an entrepreneur is a business owner with ambition.

1

Sales and customers

This is the very centre of your business, the point that the maximum possible amount of your energy should be focused on: making sales to customers.

It is the very purpose of your business, the reason why you exist now and will continue to exist in the future.

This is the excitement that will get you out of bed in the morning, will keep you working until late and will still be buzzing around in your head when you're away from work: how can we help people today, and what will we earn in return?

Successful entrepreneurs are restless. They're constantly out meeting people or seeking knowledge. They're looking for those magic connections called opportunities. What does this person want, what can that person offer, what does this information mean, and what connects all these things?

An opportunity is the beginning of a sale, and you need to be creating opportunities all the time. But this isn't magic, it comes down to planning.

TARGETING

Although this is the very first step, you'd be amazed how many businesses ignore it completely and head off blindly trying to sell to anybody.

If you don't have a clear idea of who your target customers are you'll waste a lot of time and money trying to sell to the wrong people. This exercise is a key part of the planning that will make your company better at selling to and serving your customers.

Analysing your current customers

A great way to get a clearer picture of your target customers is to spend more time understanding the customers you already have.

At this point a lot of big companies would turn to formal market research, but this is where small businesses have an advantage. You and your team are close enough to your customers to be able to chat to them at the end of a meeting, take them for a drink or simply phone them up and ask them these questions:

- Why did you choose to buy from us in the first place?

- Why did you then choose to buy from us again?

- What do our products or services do for you? (What problems do they solve? How do they make your life/work easier? How do you use them?)

- Do you buy these things from anyone else as well?

- Are there any other companies who supply this kind of product or service that you have previously bought from but no longer use – and why did you stop using them?

- What different factors will influence your decision to buy less, or more, of these products/services from us in the future?

- What are the most important things you look for when selecting a supplier?

- What else could we do that would really help you?

It's best to ask these questions in conversation rather than by sending people questionnaires, as you'll be able to follow up on answers – and everyone is more guarded when they put things in writing. Another good tip is to be like a small child and ask 'why?' questions a couple of times after they answer the main question. That will really help you to get down to the important stuff, as their first answer will always be just touching the surface of the facts and their true feelings.

One added bonus is that just by you showing this kind of interest in them and their opinions, they will be more inclined to buy from you. Now how's that for an incentive to go and ask these questions? This could be a good sales tool too.

Some people worry about asking their customers questions like these in case they simply reel off a list of complaints. But, if that does happen, it's far better that you do actually know about it so you can fix the problems before they take their business elsewhere. In reality though, if they're still your customers they're likely to be generally happy with what you do, so don't worry too much! They'll just be pleased you want to hear what they think.

Once you've done this research you'll have a good idea of what your customers want from your company, and hopefully a clear picture will emerge. If not, try dividing the results up into three groups by profitability – the top third of your customers, the middle third and the bottom third. This is often when a pattern emerges. You're obviously more interested in what the most profitable customers think!

If this still doesn't reveal a pattern, further subdivide each group into two – customers that it's a pleasure to do business with and customers who you wish you didn't have to work with. This may be because they are rude, aggressive, always trying it on, or anything else. You want to create a company that attracts more of the kind of customers that you enjoy doing business with, so it's better to listen to what that kind of customer wants more closely than the others.

Insider Knowledge

I know some entrepreneurs who won't take on any new customer that they wouldn't be happy to go for a night at the pub with, and they're much happier and less stressed because of it. This also has a side benefit – customers who are focused on price more than any other factor often turn out to be the ones who it's less enjoyable to deal with. They don't value having a good relationship with you or the quality of your work – just the money. They will be rude and ruthless in order to get that best price.

Once you've identified what your best, most profitable customers want, you're one step closer to knowing the kind of potential customers you want to target.

Defining your target customers

The good news is that those very customers who are the right existing customers for you are also a role model for the best potential customers.

You need to take what you know about these existing customers and look at common themes and characteristics to divide them into different groups – somewhere between two and ten groups, but around five is ideal to avoid getting too complicated.

You might also wish to target certain types of customer that you don't already have. For example, you might sell all your products to manufacturing businesses at the moment, but have found a potential application for them in car repair workshops. That means you need to develop a group of customers that you currently know nothing about and do some research. Start by finding out about this kind of business in your local area if possible, as that makes it easier to visit them and find out about what they do. If possible, get two or three potential customers to run pilot programmes with free samples of your product. Use their feedback and their business characteristics to help you target other similar companies.

Taking the profiles of the customers that fall into these groups, write a generic profile for a fictional customer in each group. This fictional profile should be typical of all customers in this group. Make it as realistic and lifelike as possible.

If they're individuals, make up information about their hobbies, lifestyle, family, holidays and anything else that helps you understand who they are and what motivates them. You can even go as far as to give them names and more details.

If they're companies, profile the individual who will be your key contact within these companies. Put in more detail about what they do, what the company does, who their customers are, who the other key contacts and decision makers in the company are (make up names again), what their key motivating factors are in any deal, how they do business and so on.

Make the profiles as detailed as possible, so that you and your team can refer to them by name, and picture them in your mind, whenever you are trying to categorize a new customer or make key decisions on new products or services. You should know these people as if they are your friends.

You can see a sample form for a Customer Profile on the CD-Rom in the back of this book.

Using these fictional profiles, you can now really understand each group of your customers – and that means you can see if potential customers fit into one of these groups. This knowledge will help you buy mailing lists for marketing, decide which trade shows to attend, plan new product launches, manage referral schemes and so on.

Whenever you're planning new products or services, you and your team can look at these customer profiles and get a good idea of how those groups of customers will respond.

Knowing clearly what groups your customers fall into is a key part of focusing on delivering what they want.

The next stage is to break down exactly what it is that each of these customers wants from your company. Why are you the best people to provide it to them? What are the key factors they will consider in making their decision?

It can really help to pretend to be each of these customers in turn, having a meeting and examining all of the competitors, including you, that can provide this particular service. What would you do if you were them? Remember to base your decisions only on the information available to them – not on your inside knowledge of what your company does.

After this exercise, ask yourself:

- What are the three most important factors that each customer profile considers when making their buying decision?
- For each customer profile, who are our main competitors?
- How do we rank against them?

- How good is the information we provide to that customer profile to help them decide?

- What do we need to do in order to attract more of this customer profile?

- How can we gain the loyalty of each customer profile?

Congratulations, you now have very clearly defined your target customers; you are well set up for sales success.

CHANNEL TO MARKET

Now that you know who your ideal customers are, the next stage is to review the route you are taking to reach them. You can sell directly to your customers or you can sell through distributors, resellers or retailers. Each of these methods have their advantages and disadvantages. If you are providing a service it is most likely that you will have to sell directly to customers, but some reseller channels may be open to you.

Remember that you can often have more than one channel to market. Also bear in mind that no matter how long you've been established, it's always worth considering new channels to market, so even if most of these are familiar to you, there may be some new ideas.

Direct

Selling to the end user of your products or services gives you the most control. You are in charge of every part of the customer experience and the sale itself. This can be a great advantage, as you and your team will be more passionate and committed to your product than any reseller could ever be. The challenge is that it takes a lot of time and work to find these customers and sell to them.

Selling directly to business customers

This is often known as B2B sales and can involve:

- Having a sales team visiting customers.

- The telephone – incoming or outbound calls.

- Running a specialist website selling your products.

- Trade exhibitions.

- Having premises that your customers visit.

Selling directly to consumers

This is often known as B2C sales and can involve:

- Owning a shop or chain of shops.

- Owning other premises where consumers come to you (restaurant, cinema, etc.).

- The telephone – incoming or outbound calls.

- An online shop on the internet.

- Your own events (wine tasting evenings to sell wine, etc.).

- Other people's events (country fairs, wedding fairs or events organized by consumer magazines such as the Good Food show).

- Home shopping parties (made famous by Tupperware and Ann Summers, but now used by many companies including Virgin Cosmetics). This format is generally only used to sell to women, but I think there's an opportunity to sell to men here too (if it's not openly a shopping party!). What about offering exclusive wine, whisky, brandy or other booze tasting evenings in people's own homes, that they can then buy case-loads of?

- Door to door sales visits.

We'll look in more detail shortly at how to make these routes to market work for you.

Distributors

These organizations normally specialize in a particular industry or range of products. They don't manufacture, they focus on building relationships with key suppliers and key customers. They will often be well known in the industry and already have a route to most of your target customers. This can be a very well-oiled way to get your product to market. The problem is that they may also sell your competitors' products and have no reason to push your products forward more favourably or regularly.

In most cases, distributors simply stock their warehouse (with as little stock as possible), publish a catalogue and wait for orders. You may still have to do a lot of promotion to help your product move from their shelves to your end users. You will also have to give them a substantial trade discount and very favourable credit terms – at the very least – in order to get on their shelves at all. In different industries distributors can be known as wholesalers.

Distributors will want trade terms such as:

- Discounts of anywhere between 40 per cent and 70 per cent on the standard sales price (in consumer terms, the Recommended Retail Price, or RRP), so that they can still make money when they have to give a large trade discount to retailers (see below).

- Credit terms of 60 to 90 days, simply because their customers will demand 30 or 60 days from them – but don't let this inside knowledge stop you from opening negotiations at 30!

Value Added Resellers

These are companies who often provide a specialist service to the end user of which your product is a part. They 'add value' to the products they sell by installing them, maintaining them and generally having specialist expertise.

This is a common business model in the computer industry where, for example, Hewlett Packard sell through Value Added Resellers (VARs). The VARs are often small local companies who have a loyal customer base for whom they provide a full IT support service that just happens to include the sale of HP computers when necessary. They also often sell Microsoft software and specialist software from smaller companies.

Could a VAR model work in your business? Does your product benefit from being provided alongside a service from a specialist provider? If so, then this is an excellent business model. The only problem comes from the fact that the VAR wants a nice healthy profit too, so it can make it hard to be competitively priced – as the computer industry found out when Dell entered the market and bypassed the VARs.

Resellers

These are other companies, often other small businesses, who buy your product or service at a discount and sell it on to their customers – and these are generally other businesses too. In some cases they might take a commission on any sales they make instead of a discount. This works for companies who provide a service as well as simply for those who provide products. However, this is often just a sideline for this kind of reseller and they don't make enough money from it to focus much of their time or effort on the work, often treating it as an 'upsell' to existing customers.

It can also be the equivalent of a retailer, but one who specializes in business customers – think of office supplies companies, stationery catalogues and so on.

Finally, some companies have 'affiliate' schemes, essentially offering their products or services through resellers. Amazon do this with their website.

So, to look at some examples of resellers, a local accountant might agree to sell your business training courses to their customers in return for a 20 per cent commission. Or an office supplies company might agree to sell your comfortable office chairs to its customers if you grant them a 50 per cent trade discount.

Essentially a reseller is someone who already has the relationship with the customer and sells your products or services to them in return for a share of the money.

Retailers

This is generally taken to mean a business that sells to end-user consumers. Often they will buy through distributors, but sometimes they may buy direct – particularly if they are small companies, you are an important player in your market or you are local to them.

The business terms that retailers will expect are:

- Discount. They will want a trade discount which will start at around 30 per cent, but some larger retailers will demand anywhere up to 50 per cent discount. In a few cases it can be more than this, which is shocking. Generally this is because they are really bad at running their business, so have to take a bigger share of the sales price on any product just to be able to fund their mistakes. If any retailer demands discounts of this size from you, just read up about them on the web or in the financial press and see how regularly they change chief executive or finance director, or when they last announced a 'turnaround plan'. They'll also have had years of poor financial results which they will have blamed on 'a cold summer', 'a summer heatwave', 'the war on terror', 'the world cup' or any other current event they can think of.

- Terms of sale. They will want to negotiate 'Sale or Return' terms. This means that they buy your product, but if it doesn't sell they can send it back to you and get a refund. Try to avoid this and keep them on 'Firm Sale' terms (they buy it and it's theirs until they sell it). If they insist on Sale or Return, which may be standard in your industry, then set a time limit for returns of, for example, three months. Also set a percentage limit so they can only return 70 per cent of what they buy.

- Credit. They will want 60 or 90 days – almost guaranteed! Try to keep them to 30 or 45. If they are a big chain you'll find it hard to negotiate them below 60 or 90, but do try.

When selling to retailers you need to show them how customers will know to come into their shop to buy your product. They will want to know about press coverage, advertising and so on. They also want to be able to offer special offers and promotions to their customers.

The one thing you need to know about retailers is that your aim is not to get your product on their shelves (which is hard enough), but to get your product off their shelves once it's there. That way you'll see repeat orders and a sustainable business. If the product goes on their shelves and stays there for a few weeks, it will just come back to your warehouse as returns.

CONNECTING TO CUSTOMERS

Before you can sell to any potential customer through any of your channels to market they have to know you exist, and a basic channel of communication needs to be opened. You need to use this to make your target customers aware of you and what you can do for them. This can be done in a number of ways.

Premises

If you are a retailer, a restaurant or other business with premises that your customers visit in order to buy from you, then this is obviously a prime way to raise awareness. But it can also be useful to many other businesses. How many of your target customers might drive or walk past your building? Is your signage clear enough? Is it clear what you offer? Does it promote your benefits as well as just your company name?

Once customers get to your workplace, will they find it pleasant, attractive and clean? Will they want to spend time there? Will they want to spend money? It's well worth taking some time to arrive as your customers would, waiting in reception for a while if necessary. How could the experience be improved?

On top of this, how could the sales potential of the experience be improved? Could there be sample products on display? How else can you raise the customers' awareness of what it is that you do, and why you are so good at it?

As well as using the premises to raise customers' awareness, you'll need to raise awareness of your premises if you want customers to visit. Do you have good signposts/boards outside, and on roads nearby to direct people to you? Retailers and restaurants need to catch the passing trade, so work out any way you can to draw people's attention to your premises.

Direct mail

These days it is much harder to connect with customers through direct mail (DM) as much of it ends up straight in the bin. Consumers and businesses alike are weary of the amount of post they receive each day that is of no interest to them and simply wants to sell to them by bombardment rather than benefits.

But direct mail can still be a valuable tool. The keys to successful use of DM are as follows:

1. Very precise targeting. Keep your costs down and avoid annoying people by making sure you have carefully identified your target market. Be wary of bought-in mailing lists as they can be expensive and out of date. They can also lack the careful targeting you need. Be sure to check the supplier thoroughly and perhaps buy only a small number of names at first to test the list. Also, think carefully about which of your customer profiles you are targeting with this campaign. What defining characteristics do you want to use to select a mailing list?

2. Set clear objectives. Do you simply want to let people know where you are? Do you want to promote a new product? Do you want to make sales? Think about exactly what you want the customer to do as a result of your mailing.

3. Time your campaign. When is the best time of year to run your promotion? You won't get many orders for lawnmowers in November, but customers will scramble for a special offer in March to get an 'early-bird' discount. You might need to plan your targeting based on the timing being right for the individuals – SAGA mails people who have just turned 50, for example.

4. Design with the recipient in mind. What will people think when they see your mailing on the doormat or their desk? Will they instantly classify it as junk mail and bin it? Will it look formal and businesslike so they feel they ought to open it? Your first design challenge is to persuade them to open the envelope.

The next challenge is to get them to read more than the first few words. What message will they find so interesting that they have to read on? What benefits will they get from what you are offering? A great exercise is to collect all the junk mail that you and your team receive at work and at home for a few weeks and then sort it into the good, the bad and the ugly. Look at what you think works, and what doesn't.

You may well find that a simple A5 photocopied leaflet can outgun a glossy brochure in some cases for some types of promotion. In many cases though, highly personalized letters produce much better results than just a general mailing.

Also decide whether to include any other materials in the mailing, such as catalogues, brochures or special offer vouchers.

5. Call to action. When the recipient has scanned through your carefully crafted message they should not be left wondering, 'So. . .?' They should be thinking, 'Okay, I have to fill in this form and send it back,' or 'Okay, I'll telephone them now for a quote.' It should be very clear what the reader needs to do if they are interested. Design the call to action to achieve the objectives you set for the campaign.

6. Test and develop. Every time you do a mailing, keep notes of who it was sent to, how it was designed and what the response was. Then change *one* thing the next time you do a campaign and see what effect that has on the response rate. This will help you to continually improve your direct marketing. Try changing every element, but only one at a time. Professional DM designers will try a different font, a different type of paper, different envelopes, a different headline on the letter or a different design of order form – anything is open to experimentation. The challenge is that there is no one right answer for all companies. Different target audiences respond in different ways.

7. Repeat and repeat. We human beings are pretty slow to take any kind of action, and pretty lazy. You may need to contact each customer a couple of times to get a half decent response out of the whole campaign. Try using a variety of marketing methods, such as sending them a mailing and then telephoning them to follow up on it. You'll be surprised to find quite a few people who will say something like, 'Ah, yes. I meant to get in touch with you but I forgot.' People can be very frustrating to deal with sometimes –

but then do you always respond to advertising campaigns immediately?

Some individual consumers are on the Mailing Preference Service list, meaning that they don't want you to contact them if you don't already have some kind of business relationship with them. See **www.mpsonline.org.uk** for details. Checking names against this list is only required of companies who are members of certain direct marketing organizations, so if you use a marketing agency they will do this. You don't have to do this by law.

The question that everyone wants to know when planning a DM campaign is: how many people will respond? The startling reality is that the response rates are most likely to be between 0.5 per cent and 2 per cent for a mailing to customers you haven't dealt with before. This goes up if you are mailing customers who have already dealt with you in some way.

Email newsletters

This medium is rapidly growing in terms of users – and in terms of the amount of junk mail delivered by it. This is making it more and more difficult for genuine businesses to be seen among the offers for bodily enhancement pills and porn sites. Because it is a medium based on technology, the technology is quickly being adapted to filter out this junk mail, or 'spam' as it has become known.

That means you have to work harder to get your email newsletter to reach your target audience, and once it's there you have the same challenges of getting them to open it, read past the first sentence and then take action.

However, the advantages of email are that it is cheap, and if the target user does decide to take action it is very easy for them to do that immediately before they forget. It is an instant medium, so they just click on a link or hit 'reply'.

The secrets to success are exactly the same as for DM. Target, set objectives, plan the timing (this can even be scheduled for a particular time on a particular day with email!), design for the user, call to action, test and develop – and repeat.

So how do you avoid getting banned by the spam checker? Here are some basic tips:

1. Avoid any rude words in your mailing, anywhere. This applies even to parts of words, like bum as part of a bum. This makes it difficult to show your company address if you are based in Scunthorpe.

2. Avoid sending the emails from a public use email account such as Hotmail or AOL. Send them from a proper company email like **yourname@companyname.co.uk**. You'll find some useful links to get domain names and email accounts on the FlyingStartups website.

3. Don't overuse capital letters, particularly in the subject line.

4. Avoid using spam type keywords such as 'Free'.

5. Include links to allow people to unsubscribe or subscribe to your e-newsletter.

6. Avoid sending attachments with the email, even if it's just a spreadsheet of your prices. Spam filters may automatically assume that attachments are porn or viruses, and users will be wary of opening them anyway.

7. Avoid having numbers in the email address you send from.

It's also worth taking these extra steps so that your target users recognize that your email is worthwhile and do not delete it instantly:

1. Include your company name in the 'from' address or in the subject line.

2. Make the subject clear, targeted and professional.

3. Write the body of the email in a professional way. Check your spelling and grammar.

4. Make the email short and snappy. Include links to more information on your website, as well as a link 'call to action'.

5. Include your 'real world' contact details, such as telephone number and address.

6. Only regularly send emails to people who have agreed to be on

your mailing list. Gather these agreements via your website, competitions, enquiry forms, order forms, etc.

7. If people ask to be taken off the list, take them off immediately.

Website

This is rapidly becoming one of the most important ways of communicating with customers in many industries. I know that when I'm considering buying from a company at home or at work, the first thing I do is browse their website. I have a look at the sections on their products or services, and I have a look at the 'About Us' section. Then, if I like what I see, I place my order online if I can. Are you ready to serve customers like me?

There are different types of website, including:

1. 'Brochureware'. This is just an online equivalent of your company brochure, providing pictures and text about who you are and what you do. A customer then has to telephone or email to make an enquiry or an order.

2. Portal. This is an online hub around which people with a similar interest gather. Its aim is to build a community and provide it with information. This can be very useful as a marketing tool.

3. E-commerce. This allows customers to browse through your range of products or services and place an order online with their credit card or customer account.

4. Extranet. This is used in business to business sales and allows a very small, select group of customers to access a secure website which provides in-depth information on your products and enables them to place orders and maintain their account.

Which type of website is going to be right for your business? Which will achieve your objectives? Which is within your budget (hint, I started with the cheapest and worked up)?

If you already have a website, take some time to surf through it from the customers' perspective. Does it help you get the information you need? Does it make you want to buy? Does it make it easy to buy?

If you don't have a website yet, or if you'd like to get a new website, it's time to find a web design agency. There are thousands of these, so how do you go about selecting one?

Start by asking people you know if they can recommend one. Then browse the websites of companies you know. Which ones do you like? Find out who their web designer was. Finally, you can do some research on the search engines to find design agencies near you. Study their websites to check that they know what they are talking about.

Once you have a shortlist of companies, you can contact them with your requirements in a short project briefing and ask for a quotation. When writing down your project briefing, consider the following:

1. What is the purpose of the website? Information, sales or something else?

2. Who is the target audience for the website?

3. How often will the website need to be updated? If this is going to be frequent you can save money in the long run by getting them to install a simple 'Content Management System' (CMS) so that you can update the content yourself using a simple user interface. Some web agencies will start talking telephone number prices at the mention of these three words, but simply point them to one of the free CMSs, such as **www.joomla.com**, **www.drupal.org**, or a number of alternatives which are reviewed at **www.opensourcecms.com**. These software packages are 'open source', which means that they are developed by the user community and are free to use. That's right, free. You will however need to pay your web company for their time to set them up and design the look and feel. You will also find web designers on the community forums on the websites of these software packages who will be willing to set the software up for you at a very reasonable price.

4. Similarly, if the website needs to have e-commerce facilities, take a look at some of the cheaper or free open source alternatives: **www.x-cart.com** or **www.oscommerce.org**. Again, your web agency will need to set up and design these packages – or find a web designer to do it from the community forums.

5. Specify that the website must comply with the accessibility requirements of the Disability Discrimination Act. This will also help make the website more friendly and welcoming to search engines.

6. Beware of paying extra for search engine submission or optimization. It is free to submit your website to the most important search engines. Also, the search engines are wise to a lot of the 'tricks' that overkeen web agencies use to try to boost the ranking of their clients' websites, and they will actually penalize your site, or even ban it, in the listings. If you do want specialist search engine advice then be absolutely sure to check references of the company, look at other sites they work for and get them to explain exactly what they plan to do. Don't let them try baffling you with science – it's a warning sign of cowboys. The one thing that will get your website ranked highly on the search engines is really interesting content. Focus on that.

7. Specify when the site needs to be ready by. You may want to specify milestone dates for key parts of the project.

8. Do you want them to arrange to host the site on a server or do you have your own?

The web design companies will come back with quotations, and the larger the company the larger the bill will be! Don't just choose on price though. Choose to work with someone who you think will give you the best value – a site that really works for you at the best possible price. Also, don't rule out the one-man bands working from home. Just because they don't have flashy offices with pot plants (I mean plants in pots, rather than the other kind which they might have), that doesn't stop them from being clever people – they've just made a lifestyle choice in an industry where it is very easy to work from your spare bedroom and be brilliant.

When it actually gets down to designing your site, here are some key design tips:

1. Make it very, very clear on every single page who you are and what you do as a company. It's amazing how many companies' websites fall at this first hurdle.

2. Put your postal address and phone number on every page, even if it's right at the bottom. Some people look for it and are always reassured when it is there.

3. Write clear, snappy copy.

4. Check your copy for spelling and grammatical mistakes as if it were a letter that was going to be read by millions of judgemental people (because it is going to be read by millions of judgemental people).

5. Have a clearly labelled 'About Us' section, with a bit of background about the company, your contact details and even directions for how to find you.

6. Have a clearly labelled 'Contact Us' button to allow people to email you then and there.

7. Put your logo in the top left of the page, and make it so that the user is returned to the front page of your website when they click on it – that's what they expect.

8. Make the site interesting with photos that are relevant to your business.

9. Provide other useful resources, such as articles on industry news (and the search engines will love this stuff).

When the website is ready, get lots of your friends and colleagues to spend some time testing it. Not just having a look at the front page and saying, 'Wow! That looks nice, well done,' but actually trying to use it as a customer would.

Leaflets

Let's not spend too long on this one – we both know what a leaflet is! Just be sure to think about the design from the customers' point of view, have a clear objective for what you want to achieve and have a call to action.

Trade shows

If you pick the right show, and handle it well, it can provide you with a stream of valuable contacts.

The key points to consider are:

1. Which shows are the right ones to be at? There will be some for your industry itself, but think about what other shows your target customers might attend.

2. Should you exhibit or just attend and network? Exhibiting can be prohibitively expensive for small companies – the prices are geared up to what the big companies can pay – so it may be best just to attend in the first year as a research and networking exercise, then pick one or two to exhibit at in the future.

3. Plan your objectives. Exhibitors often expect to make sales at trade shows and so go home disappointed. At most shows visitors aren't there to buy, they're there to network, learn and discover new potential suppliers and products. The sales come by following up with these people afterwards. If you bear this in mind when planning your objectives you'll get a better result.

4. Design your stand (if appropriate). How will you stand out? How will you encourage people to stop at your stand and discover what you have to offer? Think of your target customers. What would make them interested enough to spend some time at your stand? What product demonstrations can you have to raise their interest levels? What should you avoid because it would discourage them from lingering – sales people ready to pounce with order pads? How will you get their contact details so you can follow up afterwards?

5. Be warm, friendly and approachable. This means not standing on guard at the entrance to your stand, not slouching around in chairs looking bored and not all clustering in a group having a chin-wag. When you start talking to people don't say, 'Can I help you?' as they will say no and hurry away. Open the conversation as you would if you knew them socially, 'How are you enjoying the show?'

6. Have a gimmick that gets you noticed and talked about – if this fits in with your company image. This could include: wearing funny costumes and having a theme on the stand; having a 'cool' thing on your stand for people to see or play with; having something fun to give away; running an innovative competition; or providing some kind of service that people would value at an exhibition.

Advertising

This is an expensive business and will only produce results for you if you plan your campaign very carefully and really focus on one key message to get across in your adverts.

The other thing to note is that advertising is all about repetition. Running one advert in your local paper or a couple of spots on your local radio station will most likely get you a response rate of zero. Successful advertising is all about repetition. McDonald's are one of the biggest spending advertisers in the world, and it works for them because wherever you go, they get there before you. On billboards, on the bus, in magazines, on the radio. I challenge you to spend a day without seeing the golden arches or hearing mention of the name 'McDonald's'. When you start to feel a bit peckish, the chances are then much higher that you will consider looking out for a nearby McDonald's. They know better than anyone else that successful advertising is all about repetition.

But repetition is expensive, and this means that advertising may well be out of the reach of your small business. It's a waste of money to do a half-hearted small campaign, so use your budget elsewhere – or do your advertising in creative ways:

1. Buy a very small amount of advertising and then get the media to promote you for free! A few entrepreneurs I've met have a trick of only booking a few advertisements but making them controversial so that they get complaints from readers or competitors (and sometimes the entrepreneur gets their friends to complain just to be sure). This then gets picked up as a news story by the journalists we have in our media these days who think that any argument is a news story. Why not use their lack of imagination to get yourself some media coverage? But make sure that your brand is 'cheeky' enough to get away with this. The end result will be a news story about the complaints, a news story about you refusing to back down, a news story about you eventually 'giving in' and cancelling all those other adverts you had 'booked' and a news story about you inviting one of the 'complainants' to come to your office to help design the next advertising campaign. This stuff can run and run! That generates the repetition that you need for successful advertising, without the costs – but beware, unleashing the media can be a dangerous game if you don't know what you are doing.

2. Advertise in a weird place in order to get the media to promote you. There's been a bit of a trend for people auctioning off advertising space on parts of their body using eBay recently, and the media obligingly run news stories about some of these people and the adverts they are wearing. You would have your local newspaper photographers falling over themselves to get a shot if you announced that one of your attractive customers (being realistic, a friend!) was so pleased with your product that she (newspapers do prefer to photograph women) had your website address written on a publishable part of her body in a henna tattoo. If it's a slow news day the photo from the local newspaper will be picked up and used in some of the national newspapers the next day.

3. Create your own advertising. This means finding somewhere new to put your advertising so that you don't have to pay big fees to advertise there! You could have something made with your advertising on that people normally have to pay for, and so would happily take yours for free. Advertising is about repetition, so try to find as many different ways of doing this as possible, and have them in as many places as possible. This is much easier if you're targeting consumers and you have a 'cool' brand, but if you work your brain hard enough you should be able to come up with a suitable idea for almost anything. What you come up with will vary greatly depending on who your target market is.

4. If you must advertise in traditional media then be aware that the price they quote is their opening offer and is always open to negotiation. They will give steep discounts if you can move quickly and fill a big space they've got in two days' time, as they will never be able to sell that space again once the time has passed. They will also give big discounts for booking a series of adverts with them. They'll try to get you to take the biggest spaces, but smaller spaces can be just as effective. Browse through the publication and see which adverts catch your eye most.

Advertising is only worth doing if you can either be creative about it or throw a large budget at it without it sinking your company. And did I mention that successful advertising is all about repetition?

Signs

If your business depends on people finding and visiting your premises then invest in decent signs. Not just on the building, put signs wherever you can: sandwich boards on the pavement, directional signs on local signposts, signs at the end of your road, signs at the entrance to your business park – anywhere that will help people to find you.

These signs also raise awareness and can be a great advert for your business. Make sure it's clear what you do and why you're so good at it – but don't clutter them with information. Use snappy headlines.

Catalogues

For many businesses their catalogue is their main shop window. It gets sent to existing customers and distributed to targeted potential customers.

But not all businesses make use of this sales tool. Could you produce a catalogue? It will help your existing customers understand the full range of products and services that you offer and impress potential customers with your range and how well-organized you are.

Why don't accountants, lawyers, consultants and other professionals have a simple but nicely presented catalogue of their services? Most of their customers won't know half of the services they are capable of offering – and they could add products into the mix as well. Why not sell specialist books on their area of expertise? Why not sell template contracts or letters?

Catalogues can be used by nearly every type of business to help increase awareness of what they can do.

Press coverage

This is one of the best ways of raising awareness, and it's no accident that you read a lot about certain entrepreneurs in the papers. They court this publicity by arranging stunts, setting up stories and creating intrigue in order to get the journalists to write about them – and therefore their products. The media particularly like it if you're an attractive woman (they're very shallow), so if you are, use this advantage!

The media also like to have easy access to 'experts' on a range of subjects, so do keep putting yourself forward for comment. Contact the media that you would like to appear in and send them a brief summary of who you are, what you've done and why you're an expert. List the kind of topics you can comment on. Send this to individual named journalists or editors.

In the local media it may just be enough to be a general business expert – fax them a quote on Budget day, when interest rates are changed or whenever there is another big story. They'll then add your comment to the story, probably about three-quarters of the way in, along the lines of:

'Reacting to the news Bob Bingley, owner of Bingley's Ball-Bearings on the industrial estate said: "Local businesses have been expecting the bank to cut interest rates, but that doesn't make it any less welcome. For too long the interest rates have been driven by the housing market rather than by the broader economic picture."'

All it takes is typing out that paragraph and sending it by fax or email to the local paper, radio stations and any other local media.

For media coverage on specific stories about your business you will need to prepare a press release.

Tool

Press release

This is a simple document presenting your story to a journalist. Local media will often copy this almost word for word if they do publish it, but larger outlets will use this to learn the bare facts and then conduct some further interviews over the phone to get more information. They will then write an article from all the information they gather.

A press release is formatted as follows:

1. Put the words 'Press Release' or 'News Release' in big type somewhere near the top of the front page.

2. Write a headline in big type at the top of the page that neatly summarizes the story and attracts the journalists' attention.

3. Put the date that the news release was issued.

4. If it doesn't matter when the story is published put 'FOR IMMEDIATE RELEASE', or if the story mustn't be published before a certain date and time put 'EMBARGOED UNTIL (date and time)'.

5. Now write your story, with the lines double spaced and in a font that's not too small. Allow nice big margins around the side of the page. The first paragraph should cut straight to the real point of the story. Don't muck around with introductions.

6. At the end of your story put 'END'.

7. Below this put 'NOTE FOR EDITORS' and list your contact details. You can also let them know that you can provide interesting people for interview or have some nice things to photograph.

8. If you want your story to be published in a print publication you'll give yourself a much better chance if you

invest some money on a good *press* photographer (press photography is very different from portrait photography, etc.) to tell the story in a great photograph. Be creative. That means no presentations of cheques or awards. Photographs are about people, so don't just have a shot of your products – show them being used in some way. Similarly, your local TV news will want to have some nice pictures lined up for them to film or they won't be interested.

9. If you want to get your story on the radio they'll want to interview somebody in person or over the telephone. Who will give the interview and what will they say? Be prepared for this. If they visit your site what different sound effects could they record to use in the feature about you?

10. Before you send your press release out, check the spelling and the grammar. Does it read well? Keep editing it until you are happy.

Keep a list of all the media that you are interested in being in. This might include local newspapers, radio and TV, as well as trade publications or certain consumer magazines. It's also worth remembering internet sites that cover your industry.

Keep this list up to date, with details of the journalists as they come and go, and then send your press releases to a named journalist. A lot of them like to receive press releases by email now. If you do this then attach a copy as a Word file, but also copy the text into the body of the email.

Insider Knowledge

When I was a journalist I used to read the first paragraph of any press release, but if it wasn't much of a story I'd skip straight to the last paragraph, as companies or their less experienced PR agents often used to bury the real story there by mistake. So read your press release when you've written it. Have you written a nice pithy summary at the end? Good – now put that at the start.

Sponsorship

This can be a good way of getting press coverage or awareness in your local community, but what could you sponsor? A local school football team's kit? An awards ceremony?

Could you sponsor them by providing a product or service rather than actual cash?

Product placement

This form of promotion is on the rise, with product placements appearing in films and TV programmes. Next time you sit down to watch a Hollywood blockbuster see how many logos you can spot of big companies. The hero will look at his watch to see how long he has before the bomb goes off – and look, we get a nice lingering shot of it too! Next he'll hop into his fast car and we'll get a shot from just in front of the car, showing the logo while the hero stares meaningfully ahead at the road. What breakfast cereals do they have on their table? What canned or bottled drinks do they consume? What hotels do they stay in? All this is contractually arranged and paid for in order to give you a positive image of a product: 'If James Bond uses it to tell the time it must be good.'

But product placement can actually be a much more useful thing for the consumer – and more accessible to you as a small business. This happens when you place samples or demonstrations of your product in useful places for the customer to test them. The luxury soap company Molton Brown discovered this and makes its products available to hotels and restaurants of a certain class.

Where would be a good place for customers to be able to experience what you do, in a setting that gives them a good image of your company?

Awards

There are lots of award ceremonies in different industries or for business, or even entrepreneurship in general. Enter as many awards as you can because this will bring you to the attention of many potential customers.

Even being shortlisted for an award can help. You can put it on your website, in your newsletter or even on your letterhead.

Even better, journalists see award ceremonies as an easy story to write about (the two easiest stories for journalists are awards and surveys – count the mentions of each in your newspaper today to see how much of a slow news day it is!). They'll also refer to the list of award winners at a later date when they desperately need to find an expert in the ball-bearing industry at short notice. If you won 'Ball-Bearing Manufacturer of the Year' you'll get their call.

Collaboration

This is one of the cheapest, most underused tools available to small businesses. Even big companies manage to get their act together on this one, forming groups to run loyalty card schemes, so why can't entrepreneurs?

You can collaborate with other businesses in your local area, your industry or related industries in order to promote each other to your customers – and to potential customers. It's not about doing the selling for other people, it's about raising awareness.

Imagine a small local town. The hairdresser, the coffee shop and the dry cleaners decide to work together. Here's what they could do:

● Jointly produce a flyer with a promotion for each business. These could be given to customers by each business, or perhaps delivered through local letterboxes.

● Have a voucher scheme: when you get your haircut, you're given a couple of special offer vouchers to give you a free cup of tea with any slice of cake at the coffee shop plus 10 per cent off your next dry cleaning bill – valid for the next week. Each business gives out vouchers to encourage people to use the other businesses.

To exercise your collaboration thinking, what else do you think they could do?

Imagine a company that creates specialist software for lawyers to use. They could collaborate with a legal publishing firm, a legal staff recruitment agency and a legal magazine to run a number of joint promotions, create a catalogue together and so on.

Who could you collaborate with? What promotions could you run together?

The key thing about collaboration is equality and trust. This takes time to build, so start off with a fairly modest and easy to run scheme and grow it slowly.

SELLING TO CUSTOMERS

Making your customers aware that you exist is only the first hurdle; the next is to gain their interest in what you can do for them and convert this into a sale. This process can be smoother if you observe the following:

Listen

It's amazing how few companies' sales people switch into listening mode when they have grabbed the attention of a potential customer. They switch instantly into 'transmit' and reel off a list of features, benefits, case study customers and so on.

The most effective sales people begin by listening and asking intelligent questions, such as:

1. What is it that you do that means you might need us?

2. What products or services similar to ours do you use at the moment?

3. What problems are you hoping we can solve for you?

This achieves three things. First, it shows you are genuinely interested in your customer and tailoring a solution to their needs. Second, you learn information that will give you the edge over your competitors. Third, even if you don't have what the customer wants, you find out about potential new opportunities that you could develop products or services for.

Meanwhile, your competitors are going 'yada yada yada', boring the customer and learning nothing. Who has the edge?

Remember to listen to the answers once you have asked a question rather than focusing your mind to thinking about the next question.

In your questioning seek to get a better idea of the budget the customer has available, who your competitors are for this work and – most importantly – who will actually be involved in making the decision in the customer's business.

For sales to consumers you need to listen to your customers in a different way. I find surveys or focus groups ineffective because you don't tend to get a full mix of customers taking part in them, and they lack a personal connection. I tend to favour you and your management team actually getting out there and meeting customers in the place where they buy or consume your products. Some ideas:

- Could you offer your management team to do a week's work experience for your key retailers? I bet they won't have had many similar offers from your competitors!

- Start some kind of club or community around your company. This could be online, such as the online forums that beauty products retailer Lush has set up as part of its expansion into America. Go to **www.lush.com**, click on the US flag and then click on forums to see the kind of customer opinions that they get. Could something like this help you understand your customers?

- Could you run a competition akin to that in *Charlie and the Chocolate Factory*? Have some golden tickets in your products inviting consumers to an expenses- paid visit to your headquarters to find out how you do what you do, meet senior management and help shape the next generation of products – and to get some great freebies!

You also need to learn to read between the lines. Your customer will not tell you that the real motivation in the purchasing decision will be the safest option that is least likely to make them look bad in front of their boss, rather than the one that will achieve even better results than expected but carries a level of extra risk. They won't tell you that they were willing to spend more money with a competitor because the competitor runs a lovely outing for top customers to Ascot each year, and so on.

Solve problems and attain dreams

The customer won't want to buy from you simply because you gave the longest list of product features – they will want to buy from you because you had specific benefits that applied to their particular needs. Your product or service might solve a problem for them, raise their status or enable them to achieve some other reward or benefit, attaining some dream of theirs.

Therefore, once you have found out what the customer's problems and dreams are by listening, you can focus your sales effort on demonstrating how what you offer solves their problem or helps attain their dream. Common desires, stemming from problems and dreams, that motivate people in purchasing are to:

- Avoid losing money.

- Earn more money.

- Avoid wasting time.

- Avoid or improve jobs that they hate doing.

- Look good to a boss, their spouse or their friends.

- Improve their status, powerbase or level of cool.

- Have more fun.

And be ready for the fact that a key benefit of your product in a particular customer's eyes may not be a benefit that you have already spotted.

Run special offers

This is what you may need to do if there is no real differentiation or advantage to that of your product compared to your competitors. That means you're in a buyer's market and you have to compete on pricing, and what the customer gets for that price.

Try to avoid this if you possibly can, as it's a long spiral down with you running one special offer, your competitor matching it or beating it, and then it's back to you to try and better their price.

If you have to give special offers, it's best to avoid reducing the actual price you charge, instead simply increase what the customer gets for that price. This is why 'buy one get one free' offers are now more prevalent than '50 per cent off'. This means you still get the same amount of cash, but with reduced margins – which is better than getting less cash with reduced margins.

THE SALES PROCESS

So we've looked at what is involved in finding customers, connecting with them and selling to them, but we haven't yet looked at fitting this together into a process. These are the steps on the route to winning a customer who has not heard anything about your company before:

1. Get the right channel to market to reach your target customers (see above).

2. Establish a connection by using some form of basic communication with your target customers. At its most basic this is simply to make them aware that you exist and understand what you can do for them.

3. Build on this communication by listening to the customers' problems and dreams.

4. Work out if you can help them solve any of these problems or achieve any of these dreams.

5. Establish if they have the budget and find out who the key decision makers in the transaction will be, and the key influencers. These could be people who have the final say on a particular budget spend, the users of the product or a specialist in the company. In consumer sales it will be the spouse, children, parents, etc.

6. Ensure that you are communicating with all the key decision makers and influencers.

7. Prepare and present a proposal focusing on how you will solve their problems and help them achieve their dreams.

8. Seek questions and objections to help you understand any concerns or areas in which you need to provide more information.

9. Seek a decision.

10. Keep following up with the customer, seeking questions or problems that you can answer until you get a decision.

For more details about how to develop a simple sales process and techniques that make it much easier for your customers to buy from you, read *Sold!* by Steve Martin and Gary Colleran, published by Prentice Hall Business. It's also available on audio CD (published by my company, so I declare an interest, but my recommendation of the title is genuine) from Red Audio.

AFTER THE SALE

The first sale is only the beginning of your relationship with a customer. Don't feel that your job is done once they've said 'yes'.

Deliver on your promises

The pressure is now on to deliver on your promises and, more importantly, their expectations.

Lots of courses and books talk about the importance of exceeding the customers' expectations and delighting them. That's all well and good, but it's a next step. The first step that so many companies can't even reach is simply to do what you said you'd do, when you said you'd do it, for the price that you quoted.

This is more important to customers than anything. Look at McDonald's success. Do they 'delight' you or 'exceed your expectations'? No. But you do know that every time you go to any of their restaurants, anywhere in the world, you will be able to get a burger, fries and soft drink. You know exactly what it will taste like and look like, and you know roughly how long it will take and how much it will cost. They deliver on your basic expectations every single time you go in there. Therefore, you go back.

Your customers will be much happier with you if you put all your energies into being reliable and consistent. Focus on this.

Follow up

Customers will be really pleased if you check back with them after they've been using your product or service for a while. Check that you are delivering on their expectations, whether you can help them get the best out of the product, whether it is meeting their needs – and whether you can help them with anything else. Remember that the first sale is the launch pad for the second sale.

INCREASING PROFITABILITY

Earning a profit is the responsibility of everybody in your company. Everyone can play their part by keeping spending down, buying wisely and looking for sales opportunities to pass on to the sales team. But it is your sales and marketing team who can do most to increase the profitability of your business, and you should be constantly encouraging this. Questions to ask are:

1. Can you charge more for what you do?

Small businesses are often a little shy to charge decent prices for what they do. One of the most common issues I see is underpricing. They think that because they're only small they can only charge small prices – and yet the service the end customer gets is often better than that from the big players! Customers will pay more for what they value. A small increase in your prices will bring a big increase to your profits – because it will all be profit!

2. Are you giving too many discounts?

Some sales people who are either nervous in their job, not fully trained or simply lazy give away discounts left, right and centre.

Every discount given to a customer should be questioned and justified. And every discount should be accompanied by something in return. For example, 'They wanted a 5 per cent discount but agreed to pay in 14 days instead of 60' is more acceptable than 'They said we were too expensive.'

3. **Can you sell more units to existing customers?**

Some customers may use two or three suppliers to provide exactly the same product or service. If you can prove that you are reliable and give excellent service then why not ask to get more of their business? What would it take to become their sole supplier, or their preferred supplier? This can increase your sales dramatically without even having to find any new customers.

4. **Can you sell services to add to your products?**

Some companies find that they can make huge profits by adding a service to their product. This could be installing it, maintaining it, giving training to the customer's staff, etc. Again, it's the same customer, but an extra sale.

STAYING ON THE RIGHT SIDE OF THE LAW

The key laws that regulate how businesses market and sell their products or services are:

The Sale of Goods Act

The Supply of Goods and Services Act

The Data Protection Act

These laws mean:

- You must describe your products accurately in any communications, whether these are photos, text or simply conversations.

- Your products must be of satisfactory quality.

- Your products must be fit for their purpose.

- You must carry out your work with reasonable care and skill, within a reasonable time and for a reasonable charge, or within the time and charge agreed with your customer.

- You must register any databases or lists of customer information with the Information Commissioner.

- You must ensure that any data you hold on customers meets the requirements of the Data Protection Act. You must have an identified need for storing the information; it should be accurate and up to date; it must be kept securely; and it should be deleted when you no longer need it. There are other requirements such as allowing subjects access to their data.

2

CHAPTER TWO
Employing people

What sets an entrepreneurial company apart from other companies is the way the entrepreneur attracts, motivates and focuses the team to achieve more than anyone thought possible. That requires you, the company founder, to invest a lot of time and energy in developing and applying your people management skills – and at the same time having to comply with a number of regulations.

This is an area that scares many entrepreneurs. It seems like a lot of responsibility, and it is daunting suddenly to be leading other people. In this chapter we'll explore the key things you need to know to meet your legal obligations, as well as what you can do to achieve the best possible results for your team members and your business.

RECRUITING STAFF

Recruiting, motivating and developing the people in your business is your second most important contribution to your company after having conceived the initial vision. Everything else comes in lower down the list, including managing the cash. These things can be done by someone else, but building the team in the company's key stages of development can only be done by you. When you have to delegate this as the company grows, you still need to keep a close eye on the process of recruiting and developing people – and perhaps even get more involved again as the company goes through further key stages of growth in the future. Never let go of the responsibility to communicate your vision to, and to motivate, everybody in the company. If you do, your company will just become another corporate, soulless shell.

Your recruitment needs

Part of the effort that you need to put into recruitment is to make sure that you don't build a company of clones of yourself – a common mistake of entrepreneurs. We like people like us, so it's an easy mistake to make, but it is worth working harder to find a wider range of suitable people.

You can really benefit by bringing people into your company with different experiences of work – and of life. Consider different age groups, different backgrounds, and different nationalities. Also consider offering more flexible working arrangements to attract return-to-work mothers or more experienced workers who may like to semi-retire. This can help you bring much needed experience and expertise into your business.

Differences within an organization give the company a greater breadth of strengths and knowledge, making it stronger. Look at evolution in nature: the greater the difference between the DNA of two humans or animals when they reproduce, the healthier the offspring is likely to be. If the DNA is too similar then the offspring is much more likely to have physical defects or health problems. Your company is just like that – and it's in your best interests to be constantly bringing new DNA into the business.

To help you in the recruitment process write a brief summary, on one side of paper, describing the following aspects of the job and requirements for a successful candidate:

1. The job title.

2. Activities and responsibilities that make up the job.

3. Skills and personal attributes needed.

4. The experience they should have.

5. The normal hours of work. Could they be flexible? Does the nature of the job call for flexible hours?

6. How much money you are willing to pay the successful candidate. You could show a range depending on skills and experience.

7. Whether the job requires any travelling. National or international?

8. What the prospects are for career development.

9. The other benefits that come with the job.

The next thing to consider is whether this position is something you actually need to recruit a member of staff for. Alternative solutions could be provided by finding a freelancer or a consultant, using a specialist supplier or hiring a temp for a particular contract.

You now have the job description in front of you for a position you would like to fill, and perhaps even create in your company. But creating a new position in the company as it grows is a tricky decision to make, particularly when it comes to working out how to afford to create the role.

First, you may expect that bringing in the new team member will help to increase sales, either because that is part of their job, or because they will free up the time of other people whose job it is (possibly you!). Try to quantify how many extra sales could be generated.

If this will be one of your first few members of staff then don't be tempted to make the mistake of simply recruiting people to do the jobs you are scared of, like finance, sales or managing the business. At this early stage managing the business is your role; you can hire a part-time bookkeeper to manage finance, and you should really think carefully before taking yourself away from the sales role. Even if you're a bit scared of sales you'll often find that no one you recruit quite has your confidence or passion in your company, and this will come across to customers. Be honest with yourself here: are you the company's best sales person in the start-up phase?

I believe that most of the time the early stage jobs that are created in the company should be focused on the key work of the business, which is:

1. Doing whatever it is that you do. Hire people who are great at, or can be trained to be great at, carrying out the main work of the company. It is often the case that the entrepreneur is skilled in this work, which is why they started the company, but the company will never be able to grow if it depends only on the entrepreneur carrying out this role. So it's best to get out of it as soon as possible and use your skill to train other people. You want the person in this job to leave you thinking: 'Wow – they do it better than I do!'

2. Delivering service to your customers. Hire people who are great communicators and great task-finishers. These are detail people who will make sure that whatever a customer orders will get sorted out by the people who do whatever it is that you do, and then be provided to the customer on time. This could be an office manager, a customer service manager, a project manager, anything you like – but the job title in your mind is, 'The person who makes stuff happen'.

Along with your bookkeeper or accountant, this is your core entrepreneurial team in the early stages of the company. Only when you have fleshed this team out a little will you generally look to start growing the sales team.

Recruiting good sales people, who fit well into your company, will be the most difficult 'people' task that you face in growing your company – that is, after letting go of 'doing whatever it is you do' to the other people you recruited and getting out of their way.

Many sales people are driven by money and status, and that makes it difficult for them to fit into an entrepreneurial company where there is little money and little status and where the focus of the people in the company is more about the vision, the adventure and the fun.

Also, by their very nature, sales people talk a good game, and that makes it very difficult for an unseasoned recruiter to select the right candidate. It's best, if you can, to leave recruiting sales people until you are a bit more experienced and the company is a bit more stable and able to put in place a suitable rewards structure to attract the best candidates.

Of course, not all sales people are like this, and you may find the perfect one – in which case snap them up and set them to work – but make sure they deliver on their promises and don't be slow to follow up on poor performance.

Promoting your vacancy

If you decide that you do want to recruit someone to your staff, how can you go about letting people know to apply for a job? The approach will vary depending on the type or level of the job. Here are some suggestions:

1. **Use one or more recruitment agencies.** Recruitment agencies charge a success-based fee. If they find someone that you decide to recruit then they will usually take 10–20 per cent of the successful candidate's first year salary.

Insider Knowledge

As with anything, the deal with the recruitment agency is open to negotiation – and a good tactic is to arrange to pay the fee in stages. Pay half on the candidate's first day, a quarter if the candidate is still there after three months and a further quarter if they are still there after six months. That way you get time to see if the appointment works out.

2. **Use Jobcentre Plus.** This is effectively a government operated recruitment agency, with the advantage that it is free. They can also provide a range of information and services to help you with recruitment and other employment practices. See **www.jobcentreplus.gov.uk** for more information.

3. **Advertise the job in your local media.** This can be quite expensive. If you already advertise your products or services in local media then why not add a 'flash' across the advertisement promoting the fact that you are now recruiting? It's also well worth considering any very-local media, such as village newsletters if you're in a rural area, parish newsletters, neighbourhood watch newsletters and so on.

4. **Advertise the job in the trade press.** If you need someone with specialist industry experience then this can be the best place to advertise. Remember that not all the trade press puts out an actual magazine, some are only online, so it's worth doing a web search to find all the options.

5. Advertise the job on recruitment websites. There are a number of job sites on the internet, some of them covering general recruitment, others specialising in particular industries.

6. Advertise the vacancy yourself. Put information about the job on your website, in your newsletter, on the footers of all your company's outgoing email, in your windows, or on your company vehicles. Advertising that you are growing and recruiting is also a great advert for your business.

7. Put the word out via your network. Get out to more events and meetings than usual and tell everyone there about the kind of people you are looking for. Ask other members of your team to put the word out to their network and their friends. Some companies even offer a reward to existing staff members if they are responsible for introducing a successful candidate.

8. Contact local universities and colleges. Students are always looking for part-time work to help fund their studying (and their lifestyle!), and they are often also interested in work over the summer period when you might want someone to fill in for staff holidays. But if you're looking for a more permanent recruit then bear in mind that students in their last year will be trying to find a job to go to when they finish their studies. You'll probably have a few thousand job seekers in a one mile radius of a university between March and July every year!

9. Include information with your products. You know the people buying your products or services like them, so might they also like to be part of making or providing them?

10. Approach people you admire. If there are any people that you have already spotted as having great potential then why not suggest that they apply? Or perhaps there is a company that you admire and you could approach some staff there?

These are just some of the ways to let people know about your job vacancy, but it's more than likely that the perfect person for you doesn't currently think they want to change jobs. They might not be reading the job ads or applying to recruitment agencies. They're simply getting on with their work, oblivious to the fact that an amazing opportunity awaits them at your company. How can you reach these people? Creativity.

Picture the ideal person for the job. What would they currently do with their time? Where will they socialize? Where might they work now? What might they read? What radio stations might they listen to? What other media might they consume? Where do they get their lunch? How could you get a message to people in any of those places? Some of the ideas listed above can be used in this situation, but here are some others:

- Small adverts on the mirrors in your local hairdresser.

- Cards on the tables in local cafes.

- Printed beermats in local pubs

Insider Knowledge

Be aware that anything you write in the advertisements for the job, or in any of the other information you provide to applicants, will count as part of an implied contract with the successful candidate from the point at which they accept your job offer unconditionally. This is unless you put in place a formal contract with a clause that states something to the effect that the formal contract 'is the full agreement between the employer and the employee and replaces any previous agreements or terms whether express or implied'.

In your adverts you will ask interested people to contact you for an application pack. In this pack you should include some outline information about your company, its products or services and your vision for the future. Perhaps also include a brief letter from one of your existing members of staff about what it is like to work in the company. You should also include an application form with some key questions that you want to ask. In addition to the necessary personal details, these might include:

1. What experience do you have in the kind of work this position involves?

2. What skills and talents do you have that may be useful in the job?

3. What makes you happy with your job? Why?

There may also be other questions that you feel are particularly relevant for the kind of position you are trying to fill.

Keep the application form as simple as possible, as some good candidates may be put off by what seems to be a bureaucratic company.

CVs are standard to ask for, and can be useful to an extent, but are generally so polished and standardized that they don't provide you with much of an insight into the person. The answers to the questions on your application form will hopefully build up more of a picture of each applicant.

If you're seeking to attract creative people, perhaps to a PR agency or advertising agency, then get them to do something creative in their application – write a short story imagining a day's work at your company, paint a picture, anything you like.

Selecting candidates for interview

The recruitment process varies according to the level of the post to be filled. Higher level jobs generally require two interviews (sometimes more), whereas lower level jobs can often be filled after one interview. The first stage interviews and generation of a shortlist can be handled by a good agency if they are properly briefed, which can save you a lot of time. The problem is that good agencies are thin on the ground and expensive in cash terms – although your own time is just as scarce a resource!

For a single interview process you want four to six candidates. Remember some will drop out, some will not want the job and some won't meet your criteria, so retain a second string just in case. For the two-stage interview process choose eight to ten, from which the first interview will produce a shortlist of three to four.

Do not delay. You should aim to select eight to ten candidates for the first interview as quickly as possible. They will be looking at other opportunities and one or more will drop out before you get to see them.

Hopefully you've had a good response to your job adverts, and now you have to decide on a shortlist of candidates to invite for interview. This is best done using a decision grid.

Tool

Decision grid

A decision grid is where you write down the names of the things or people you are trying to decide between along the top in separate columns, then down the left hand side you list the things that are important to you in making the decision.

You also include a column for 'weighting'. This is the score you give to each factor in the decision, based on how important you think that factor is. Use a number between 1 and 10.

You then give each thing a score under each factor and multiply that score by the weighting.

So, let's say you are using a decision grid to choose cheese to serve at a dinner party. (I don't suggest you really do this as people will think you've really lost it. This is just an easy example.)

You are trying to choose between Brie, Stilton and Cheddar. You decide that the important factors in your decision are how posh the cheese is seen to be (it is a dinner party after all), how ready the cheese in the supermarket is to eat, what price the cheese is and how much you like the cheese yourself.

So a decision grid based on this would look like this:

Factor	Weighting	Brie	Stilton	Cheddar
Poshness				
Ready to eat				
Price				
Like				

You now need to give a weighting to each factor based on how important it will be in your decision. Use numbers between 1 and 10 – the higher the number, the more important the factor:

Factor	Weighting	Brie	Stilton	Cheddar
Poshness	7			
Ready to eat	8			
Price	4			
Like	6			

So, in this case, it's more important that the cheese will be ready to eat and less important what it costs. You rate whether your friends will think it's posh higher than whether you actually like it. You're so middle class.

The next step is to give each cheese a score under each factor:

Factor	Weighting	Brie	Stilton	Cheddar
Poshness	7	8	7	2
Ready to eat	8	3	7	9
Price	4	2	2	7
Like	6	8	5	2

So:

● The Brie is posh, not ready to eat, expensive, but you really like it.

● The Stilton is fairly posh, reasonably ready to eat, expensive and you don't mind it.

- The Cheddar isn't very posh, but is ready to eat and fairly cheap, but you don't like it much.

You then multiply this score by the weighting to get the final score:

Factor	Weighting	Brie	Stilton	Cheddar
Poshness	7	8x7=56	7x7=49	2x7=14
Ready to eat	8	3x8=24	7x8=56	9x8=72
Price	4	2x4=8	2x4=8	7x4=28
Like	6	8x6=48	5x6=30	2x6=12

You now have weighted scores for each cheese under each factor in the decision. The next thing is to add them up:

Factor	Weighting	Brie	Stilton	Cheddar
Poshness	7	56	49	14
Ready to Eat	8	24	56	72
Price	4	8	8	28
Like	6	48	30	12
TOTAL		136	143	126

So, the Stilton wins.

Decision grids are a great way of making complex decisions between a number of things, based on a number of different factors. Use them when you next buy a computer, a car or a stereo system – they'll be a great help! They'll also be very useful in other areas of your business.

To use a decision grid in this case, list your required attributes for the job down the left hand side and the names of the applicants along the top.

You may also decide to add some further scoring factors down the left hand side such as likeability, ability to fit with your current team, or just your 'gut feel' for each candidate.

Interviewing candidates

Remember that a job interview is as much about you selling your company to the candidate as it is them selling themselves to you. People always have a choice about who they want to work for. This means that you should have some information about your company that you can send out to the candidates in advance. You should also allow plenty of time for questions from them in the interview.

But, during the part of the interview where they tell you about themselves, give them plenty of time to speak – and *listen* to what they say. It's so easy to ask a question and then spend the time that they are answering it thinking about what the next question is going to be, without really taking in what they are saying. To help avoid that it's worth writing down a list of your key questions in advance for each candidate.

In a two-stage process, the main objective of the first interview is to find three or four candidates who could do the job, fit into the culture and who seem keen. The second interview is to find which of these is best suited to your vision of the company.

The first interview should be simply structured:

- Greeting – pleasantries; help them to relax.

- Introduction – a bit about the job and why their application interests you.

- Development – enlarge on the information in their application; fill in the gaps; find out why they want to leave their current job. The objective is to ensure that you have the same range of knowledge of each candidate.

- Assessment – if there are skills to be tested, do it here. Get the candidate to sell themselves relative to the job on offer. Find out about their qualifications, abilities, talents and experience. Challenge some points and, if appropriate, put the candidate under a little pressure.

- Questions – what does the candidate want to know about the company and the job?

- Prospects – outline potential prospects for such a candidate; explore how they fit with the candidate's own ambitions

- Conditions – pay, fringe benefits and conditions of appointment. If appointed, when could they start?

It can really help to have one or two colleagues sit in on the interview with you – but not too many or it'll be daunting for the candidate. The person who will be their team leader should be there, and it's also a great idea to involve one of the team members. Prepare for the interviews in advance with these people and ensure that each understands their role.

You may also want the candidate to carry out some practical exercises as part of the interview. For example, if you're recruiting a PA or secretary you might get them to write a business letter from some outline notes, demonstrating their use of a word processor, their business writing style and their speed.

It's important to give each candidate an equal chance. This means that each interview should follow a similar planned format and should be equally challenging. If a candidate is nervous in the first few minutes give them some time to warm up and relax before writing them off.

There are some questions that the law says you cannot ask in order for the interviews to be fair for all candidates. These are questions that could discriminate between candidates on grounds other than their attitude, talent and experience. So think carefully – if it's not a question you'd naturally ask every candidate it's probably not one to ask any candidate.

Tool

Sample questions for interviews

What most interests you about the opportunity of working here?

What have you most enjoyed in your previous work?

What is your proudest achievement?

What personal qualities do you think you have?

Can you tell us about something you did in your previous job that demonstrates ....? (Insert characteristic or skill that you want them to have here.)

What has been the most difficult decision in your working life and how did you make that decision?

After each interview, write up some brief notes and score the candidate on another decision grid. Do this before you see the next candidate, otherwise they will all merge together in your mind!

Selecting the right candidate

You will now have two decision grids for each candidate, so the first task is to look for any differences between the two. Did they come across better in person or on paper? Did your view of them improve when you met them?

You'll also have some notes from the interview.

As soon as possible after the last interview, you and your fellow interviewers should get together and go through your notes and scores for each candidate in turn.

At first (or only) interview stage you should be able to weed out candidates that you all feel are weaker than the others. Now you will have a shortlist. Give each person on the selection panel a chance to summarize their feelings about each person on the shortlist and name their preferred candidate(s).

If you're agreed, congratulations! If not, then reject any candidates that don't have a member of your team supporting them and focus on the remainder. Discuss their strengths and weaknesses. Discuss how they would fit into the current team. Discuss how they might grow and develop within the company. And do allow your gut feeling to come into the discussions, but watch out for your tendency to like people like you – avoid the clones! If need be, do one final decision grid for each remaining candidate. Finally, after the only interview or the second interview, it must come down to a decision.

Welcoming your new team member

Now that you have selected your candidate, let them know by telephoning first and then following up with a letter. You should state:

- Any conditions on which your offer relies, such as 'subject to satisfactory references'; 'subject to proof of qualifications'; 'subject to passing a medical examination' (get advice before demanding this); 'subject to passing a criminal records check' (again, get advice in this case); 'subject to eligibility to work in the UK'. Also state any action that they should take to meet these conditions.

- Whether a probationary period applies (making it easier to part company after, say, three or six months if the match does not turn out to be a good one).

- The job title or description of their work.

- The date the employment will start.

It is also in your best interests to set out the agreed details with regard to pay, holidays, benefits and so on. Although this legally doesn't have to be presented in writing to the candidate yet, it can help to avoid misunderstandings or arguments.

You should send them two copies of this letter, and ask them to sign both and return one copy to you in order to accept the offer. Once they have met any conditions that you set out you should send a further, unconditional, letter of appointment.

Once you have received an acceptance of your offer you should also write to (and perhaps also telephone) the rejected candidates, along with a brief explanation – send them away with a very positive view of your company. You may also choose to file away the details of some people you think may be worth contacting about other jobs in the future.

The next stage is to prepare to welcome your new recruit to the company. This is crucial. If they don't feel welcomed and excited then they will soon start looking for other work. Help them to settle in well and they will work harder and show more loyalty. The way that you communicate with and support them in this early period will shape their attitude to your company and their view of what is expected of them. If it is friendly, thoughtful and well prepared, it implants in their mind the fact that you have to be friendly, thoughtful and well prepared to work for your company – so make sure you demonstrate the attitudes of your company very clearly.

These are my recommended steps for success:

1. Send the offer letter with a welcome pack. The welcome pack could include a brief introduction to each person in the company or team no more than a dozen people), some marketing literature (so they can get to know your products and services better) and anything else that will help them to hit the ground running on their first day.

2. Appoint a buddy – someone from the team they will be working in (preferably at the same level as them). Give the buddy some spending money to meet them for lunch one day, or drinks one evening, in the weeks before they start working for you.

3. Send them a Contract of Employment – see 'Employment and the Law' below. Send two copies, one to sign and return to you, the other to keep. A template Contract of Employment is included on the CD-Rom. This is a very important document. You should adapt the document to your needs and then get it checked by your lawyer. The template will save you time and money, but it isn't intended to replace specialist professional advice entirely.

4. Plan what the format will be for their first week. Will they shadow other people? Will they get any formal training? Who will they meet? Remember to plan in a tour of the building, including the location of first aid kits, fire escapes, fire extinguishers and other health and safety related information.

5. Telephone them a week before they start work to check that they have all the information they need, answer any questions they have and so on. Chat through what the dress code is, what the arrangements for lunch are (if there's nowhere nearby to buy food they will need to know to bring lunch with them), what the arrangements are for parking and all sorts of other practical details – plus what the format of their first week will be.

6. If they're going to need business cards, get these prepared in advance. It's amazing how exciting it is to have your own business cards on your first day! Just make sure you spell their name correctly! (I'm not kidding, this happens.)

7. Make sure their desk or workplace is clean, tidy and welcoming.

8. It's also great to have some traditions that you always observe on the first day for each new team member. Perhaps you serve everyone a glass of champagne at lunchtime or lay on a nice lunch for everyone. Make it different to normal days, and make it fun.

9. Their buddy should always be around to help them or answer questions. Perhaps you could pay for the buddy and new team member to go to lunch once a week for the first month?

10. You should meet your new team member in private at the end of the first week, the first month and the first quarter, to check how they are settling in, answer their questions and give them guidance. Do give them positive feedback on the things that they are already doing well. Build them up, but also help them in areas where they are not yet fully confident or successful.

EMPLOYMENT AND THE LAW

In many businesses the pace of work and the demands on the founder are such that proper contracts of employment don't get put into place until the business grows a little larger and begins to formalize its procedures. But that doesn't mean there is no contract of employment. For a start you must, by law, provide a minimum statement of employment, and then there are terms that become implied in the absence of a proper contract.

There are also a range of legal obligations and regulations that business owners must observe when employing people.

Written Statement of Employment

It is a legal requirement to provide all new employees with a minimum of a Written Statement of Employment within two months of starting work with you (if they work for you for more than a month), but it's good practice to give it to them in advance of their first day. It must include:

- Your company name (both in its full legal form and any trading name).

- The employee's full name.

- The date on which their employment with you began or is to begin.

- If their employment with a previous company is being treated as being 'continuous' with this job (if you bought the company they previously worked for), then the date on which that employment began.

- How their pay will be calculated, when it will be paid and what their pay rate will be.

- Their hours of work.

- What holidays they are entitled to, including bank holidays.

- What their job title will be.

- The address that will be their place of work. This may be more than one location, in which case this should be described, and your main office address should also be given.

- Who in the company they should take a complaint to (a name or a job title) and how they should make this complaint.

- Who they should complain to if they wish to complain about any disciplinary or dismissal decision against them, and how they should make this complaint.

The employee must also be provided with the following information, which can be placed in this written statement, or in a staff handbook that all employees must have a copy of or access to:

- Company rules regarding sickness and injury. This should include any provision for sick pay (which may just be that the company will pay statutory sick pay).

- The duration of the employment if the position is temporary or fixed term.

- Details of the notice periods to be given by either you or the employee to terminate the employment.

- Details of any pension schemes, plus terms related to these. This should include whether their employment is covered by a pensions contracting out certificate.

- Details of your company's disciplinary rules.

- What your disciplinary or dismissal procedures are

- Whether the terms of the employment are affected by any collective agreements with a trade union.

- Any terms that will apply if the employee needs to work outside the UK for more than one month.

Contract of Employment

Instead of simply relying on the basic written statement required by law, it is highly advisable to have a full Contract of Employment, accompanied by a staff handbook. This can help to prevent disagreements and to provide an easier resolution to any disputes that do arise.

Insider Knowledge

It is advisable to put as much of the detail as possible in the staff handbook rather than the Contract of Employment, as you have to go through a formal procedure to change or update anything in the contract, but the handbook can be changed at your discretion.

A proper and clearly defined Contract of Employment can also avoid the muddying of the waters by things you said at interview or in the job advertisement, or just things that the employee was led to believe by situations involving other employees that otherwise could still become part of the unwritten, but legally binding, contract.

It is well worth the initial expense of drawing up a proper employment contract and having it checked by a lawyer.

If you ever want to change the terms of the Contract of Employment for any employee you should also consult a specialist lawyer before taking action.

A sample Contract of Employment is included on the CD-Rom.

Keeping on the right side of the law

Recruiting and employing people is an area where there are laws to protect individuals from unfair treatment, and you need to be sure to observe these:

1. You cannot discriminate against a candidate on the grounds of disability, race, sex or marital status at any point during the selection process or during their employment.

2. You may only positively discriminate on recruitment in some specific cases – for example, if you are running a Spanish tapas restaurant and you want to employ Spanish people, or you are recruiting someone to look after elderly women in a residential

home and you want to hire a woman for the job to respect your residents' privacy and decency.

3. At job interviews, appraisals or disciplinary hearings, be careful about asking any questions relating to a candidate's personal circumstances.

4. Be aware that, under the Data Protection Act, the candidate or employee can ask to see any information you hold about them.

5. The people you recruit must be eligible to live and work in the UK.

6. You must have employer's liability insurance. Seek quotes from your local broker.

7. The maximum length of the average working week is 48 hours (excluding lunch breaks), unless your team members have voluntarily offered to opt out of this. People who are allowed to set their own hours of work are excluded from this 48-hour limit.

8. You must give a minimum of four weeks' paid holiday a year, but this can include bank holidays.

9. Part-time team members' annual leave is proportionate to the amount of days they work each week.

10. You must pay employees rates that meet or exceed the National Minimum Wage.

11. Under the Disability Discrimination Act you must be prepared to make 'reasonable adjustments' to make your workplace, or the requirements of the job, more suitable for a disabled person. This could include flexible working hours, providing special equipment and installing ramps or other alterations. You may sometimes be justified in refusing to make adjustments, including if they would cost more than you could afford, if they would not be practical or if they would not improve the ability of the person to do the job.

12. You must give every team member a written statement of your disciplinary and grievance procedures in their contract, staff handbook or welcome pack.

13. If an employee is about to, or has recently, become a parent then you must allow them maternity, paternity or adoption leave, for which they will be entitled to receive Statutory Maternity or Paternity Pay. This is a set amount per week that the government specifies, but this will be refunded to you by HM Revenue and Customs (HMRC) through the PAYE system. Small companies will also receive an additional compensation payment from HMRC. This means that, at the most basic level, you are not paying employees who are on such a statutory scheme. However, it is good practice for the employer to pay the member of staff above this very basic level – and this can be vital in retaining and motivating valuable members of staff.

14. You must also allow parents to take unpaid parental leave of up to a total of 13 weeks during the first five years of each of their children's lives. You can postpone this leave for up to six months if it comes at a critical peak time for your business, or would otherwise be too disruptive. If this leave is of less than four weeks they must be allowed to return to the same job. For longer periods it is acceptable for you to provide any job with similar or better status, pay and other terms on their return.

15. Employees who have children aged under six years (including newborn babies), or who have disabled children aged under 18, have the right to ask for a flexible working pattern, such as job-sharing, term-time working, flexitime, part-time or just slightly different hours. You must give this request serious consideration, and you can only reject the request if there is a clear business reason for doing so. You must meet with them within 28 days of their request to discuss it and write to them with your decision within 14 days of the meeting. They then have 14 days to appeal against your decision if necessary.

16. You must offer workers on flexible working patterns the same benefits, pro rata (in proportion), as you offer to full-time staff unless you can demonstrate that this is not practical for particular benefits.

17. You must ensure that the working environment is safe and secure.

18. Staff have the right to join a trade union and not be penalized for this.

In general, employment law is fair and reasonable in this country, striking a suitable balance between the needs of the employees and the needs of the employer. If you have good advisers, or if you are prepared to read up on the subject, you should have no problems.

For more advice on employment law the government has provided a useful, but little known, website at **www.tiger.gov.uk**. You can also access more details at **www.businesslink.gov.uk**, where they've really got their act together to provide an excellent site, complete with useful step by step guides.

LEADING THE TEAM

As the founder you will be expected to play a leadership role, at least in the early years of the company's growth. But what is leadership?

Fundamentally it's about having a very clear and focused vision of what the company does, what it stands for and what it's aiming for. Then it is about communicating this to the team and motivating them towards this goal. You will provide such inspirational enthusiasm and energy that your team will be fired up to go there with you. You will be an ambassador for your company and a figurehead within it.

Management is about the smooth running of a group of people. It's about delegating tasks, supervising the management of projects, recruiting people, planning the development of their talents, setting targets, reviewing targets, dealing with problems, settling arguments and sometimes disciplining people.

Successful organizations need to have both a leader and a manager, but it's rare that one person can fulfil both roles effectively. Many successful leaders hate the idea of meeting with their team to discuss pay rises or listen to grievances. Many successful managers are terrified about standing up in front of everyone and giving a motivational speech to rally the troops ahead of a big project.

Think carefully about your business and yourself. Can you really handle both roles?

In some companies you may choose to split the roles between two founders or directors, simply because it's rare for a great leader and a great manager to come packaged as one person.

But, a word of caution: if two of you split these two roles between you, don't think that will make everything rosy. The tricky part is that you both then have to act as if you are two halves of the same person. You must be working with the same attitudes towards the same focus. Otherwise your team will get mixed messages, and the unscrupulous will try to play you off against each other. Think about when you were a child. You knew what your mother would let you get away with and you knew what your father would let you get away with, so you selected who you asked based on what you wanted. Your staff have to know that they would get the same answer, and the same treatment, from either of you. This is not a good cop, bad cop routine. You are united.

If you want an illustration of this partnership of a leader and a manager working together, I urge you to watch a few episodes of *The West Wing* on TV or DVD. Examine the relationship between the president and his chief of staff (Leo). The president is a leader; the chief of staff is a manager. They share the same attitudes and focus but they can disagree and debate in private on how to achieve their aims, whilst presenting a united front to the outside world. There is a deep respect between them as they fulfil their different roles. Their team know who to go to in each case and that the answer they get will be definitive. The manager is led by the leader, but equally the leader is managed by the manager. It is a balanced relationship based on respect at all levels.

If you are a leader, who is your chief of staff? If you are a manager, who will be your president?

If you really think you can take on both roles then make sure you can balance them both and that you don't end up doing more of one than the other.

To help you develop your leadership skills I recommend *How to Lead* by Jo Owen, published by Prentice Hall Business.

MANAGING STAFF

When managing your team it's important to remember that everybody is different and will need to be managed in different ways. Some people like to be told what to do, to do it, and then to have someone to report back to about how well they've done it. They then like that person to tell them how well they've done and give them something else to do.

Other people like to be a bit more in charge of their own time, simply being given a big project to do and left alone.

Your job as a manager is to understand each member of your team and to manage them as individuals. It is your responsibility to adapt to their needs, not their responsibility to adapt to yours.

As a manager you will be there to help them access the training and support in order to develop new talents and take on new responsibilities.

On top of that you'll be there to help with the controls of the organization – approving expenses, annual leave requests and so on.

But there's more: you will be responsible for hearing complaints, resolving problems and disputes.

Many entrepreneurs start their businesses after leaving large organizations, and they are very disenchanted with 'management'. They probably fell out with their manager, felt their talent and ambition were too restricted by managers, or that managers were simply there to get in the way. It's important to realize that what's at fault here is not the art of management, but rather the people and the organization who are practising it very badly.

I had a bad manager at one stage when I worked for a big company. It's taken me years to separate that bad experience because of an organization and certain people, from the thought that management is a bad idea. For most of the years running my company I've tried to get away with just being an okay leader and ignoring the management role, convinced we'd be better off without it. But I've gradually realized that this was a mistake and that having proper management in place could make the company stronger – and a much better place to work.

The kind of management that you decide to operate in your company will vary depending on the industry you're in and the kind of culture you want your company to have.

At a basic level though, it's worth putting these systems in place:

1. Set simple, clear policies on booking annual leave, taking sick leave, booking business travel, claiming expenses, etc., and have very simple forms for each case.

2. Ensure that your team have up to date employment contracts. A sample contract is given on the CD-Rom accompanying this book. Use this as a template to develop your own, but do have it checked by your lawyer.

3. Each year you should develop personal objectives with each team member. These objectives are of two kinds. The first is operational responsibilities and the second personal development. In an entrepreneurial organization every member of staff must be on an upward curve of continuous development.

4. Hold a quarterly, or half yearly, meeting with each member of your team to review progress against their objectives and to discuss current projects, potential training and any challenges they'd like to have a go at. Through the discussion you should help each team member to identify the relative strengths and weaknesses they have shown in the course of their work. Avoid the temptation to be the first to identify a strength or a weakness. Listen to them. Reinforce the successes and the strengths. Help them get the weaknesses or failures into perspective if they are overly self-critical. If they do not identify weaknesses that seem apparent to you, ask them about them. Don't challenge or criticize. It is important to stress that there should be no comparisons with other people. This may identify a training need or simply provide more of a focus in a neglected area. Praise is good but don't patronize. This meeting should also be two-way. Have they got any comments or concerns about your management?

5. Have a file for each member of your team. As well as using this to store their contact details, information on their next of kin, their

objectives and reviews and their contract, you should also have a calendar on a sheet of paper to record annual leave days, days off sick, etc.

6. Have a leave chart on the wall in each team area so that people can co-ordinate days off, holidays, etc. to avoid overlap, and so that they are aware of booked leave for other team-mates.

7. Study proper health and safety regulations for your line of work and ensure that these are put into action in your company.

8. If someone is doing something badly wrong then take them aside for a quiet word straight away. But for small mistakes, people will normally be self-critical enough without you adding any pressure.

9. Knowledge and expertise is a valuable resource in any company, and it is part of the manager's role to ensure that it is shared and, as far as possible, recorded. Part of this is ensuring that everybody in the company has someone who can stand in for them if necessary. Confidential information should be carefully safeguarded, and those members sharing the knowledge should be aware of the appropriate security procedure.

10. Your team should also be made aware of the need for general security of information. There will be people who want to know about your operation – competitors, suppliers, or just marketing companies. Make sure they only get information that you want them to have. Brief your staff members on this.

Delegation

As an entrepreneur your business is your baby, which makes it very hard to let go of important parts of the work. One of the hardest lessons to learn is to delegate, but once you try it for a while you'll be surprised to find that people are often better at things than you. Even though they may do things differently – and you have to let them do this – the results are often the same or better.

People need some freedom in their work, they need responsibility and they need to feel trusted.

At first you'll begin by delegating tasks: 'Can you prepare a quote for so-and-so for 1,000 units of thingamyjig please.' But gradually, as you learn to trust and see the growth of your team, you'll learn to delegate responsibilities: 'I'd like you to take charge of the stock system and making sure we always have enough to cope with a month's worth of customer orders, and that suppliers deliver the orders on time and in good condition please.'

This is when your business will really start to fly – the more areas of your business that can run without your day to day involvement, the more successful you will be.

REWARDING STAFF

Different people seek different mixes of rewards for their work. Some people are entirely money focused, while some place a high importance on feeling they are doing valuable and important work, and some value flexibility and freedom. Some want to fulfil ambitions, some want nice perks and some want the reward of pride in themselves and their work.

Financial rewards can include:

- Pay (I think you can count this one as a certainty!) See Chapter 3 for information you need to know about paying staff.

- Commissions on sales.

- Bonus on reaching specified performance targets, either individually or as a team or company.

- Profit sharing (employees share a certain percentage of the company's profits each year).

- Having shares in the company (we'll look at this in more detail shortly).

Other parts of a rewards package can include:

- Company car.

- Discounts on company products or services.

- Discounts negotiated with other companies.

- Part-time/flexible working hours (ideal for return-to-work mothers).

- Entertainment/travel (the chance to travel to trade fairs, see customers, etc.), plus

Other things that people value highly in their work can include:

- The freedom to come up with their own ideas and implement them.

- Being made to feel valuable and valued within the company.

- Feeling that their work is important.

- Having the opportunity to learn and develop new talents.

- Variety in their working life.

- Pride in what the company does.

- Friendly workplace, with colleagues they look forward to spending time with.

In fact these are often the most important rewards in recruiting and retaining talent in a small business. Large companies can throw money at people, but they find it very hard to give these other, non-financial, rewards.

To develop the rewards structure for your business, mixing and matching from the lists above and your own ideas, you'll need to take into account:

1. The industry you are in. If you're in the film industry, chances are that most of your team will be motivated more by fulfilling their ambitions and the love of their work than simply by money. In the ball-bearing industry it might be a little different. You'll also need to take into account other industry expectations, deciding either to go along with them or to make a conscious decision to buck the trend.

2. The kind of company you are. If you are aiming to be a caring company then reflect that in the way you reward your talent. If you claim to be an innovative company, develop some innovative awards.

3. The characteristics of the people you want to recruit and retain. Certain types of people favour certain types of rewards. Think about the ideal people you would like to attract to your company. What is really important to them? What stage of life are they at? What is their focus, their attitude? What motivates them?

Rewarding with shares

Using your company's shares to reward key members of your team, or in some cases all of your team, is incredibly powerful – nothing can match a sense of ownership as a motivator. But it's complicated and can be costly.

You definitely need legal and accounting advice to explore this route. There are some standard schemes approved by HM Revenue and Customs, such as the Enterprise Management Incentive Scheme, and I know of companies that have used these with great success.

Among other issues, you'll need to consider:

- Taxation issues – so that neither you nor your team get hit with big tax bills as a result of implementing the scheme.

- Whether the shares carry voting rights, and therefore a level of control in the company, or are simply there as a financial reward.

- Whether you will grant shares (give them away), sell shares (get the team to buy into the company, possibly at a discount) or grant options (the right to buy shares at a fixed price on a future date, when hopefully they will be worth much more than that).

- What will happen to the shares if a team member leaves the company.

Pensions

If you have five or more employees then you must provide access to a stakeholder pension scheme, unless you already offer an alternative pension scheme for all employees to which you contribute at least 3 per cent of the basic pay for each employee.

You do not have to make contributions to a stakeholder scheme, just make it available to your staff. Most large financial organizations offer a stakeholder scheme. Seek a number of proposals before deciding on one for your company.

It's then up to employees to set up their own pension under the scheme with the provider you have selected, but you must make any necessary deductions from their payroll and pay them into their pension.

While the stakeholder pension is a required minimum, full pension schemes can be a highly valued reward, and some people may see them as a requirement of any job they would take. They can help you to attract and retain staff.

You can find more information at: **www.thepensionservice.gov.uk** and **www.stakeholderhelpline.org.uk**.

Some other ideas

Here are some interesting ideas for rewarding people that I've seen or heard about:

- A highly successful software company chartered a jumbo jet and flew their team, along with their families, out for a weekend in the sun.

- I've heard of a couple of companies organizing annual team picnics or barbeques, with families invited.

- One soft drinks company organizes a small music festival with local bands to reward their staff, entertain their customers and build their relationship with the local community, all in one event!

- Microsoft reward their staff with shares, and claims to have more millionaires than any other company.

PROVIDING A SAFE WORKPLACE

All companies must carry out a Risk Assessment. This involves touring your premises to look for any potential hazards, evaluating the risks, deciding how to minimize the risks and recording these findings.

Potential risks include tripping, slipping over, falling, fire, electrical shock and moving machinery and vehicles.

Your Risk Assessment needs to pay particular attention to the measures you have in place to deal with fire, including the availability of fire extinguishers, the practice of fire drills, the fire alarm testing procedure and whether your building meets fire regulations.

You must:

- Have an official accident book to record any incidents.

- Display your certificate of employer's liability insurance.

- Display the poster 'Health and Safety law – what you should know' or hand out the leaflet of the same name, which you can download as a PDF from **www.hse.gov.uk/pubns/law.pdf**.

You can get further information on Health and Safety at work from the Health and Safety Executive at their website, **www.hse.gov.uk**.

You must also provide a clean workplace, particularly the toilets and any kitchen facilities. The workplace should also be comfortable with regard to temperature.

WHEN STAFF LEAVE

One of the hardest moments in the career of any entrepreneur is when a member of staff leaves. It's almost impossible not to take this personally. But it happens, so in true entrepreneurial style let's make the best of it.

Basic steps

- Ask the staff member to confirm their resignation in writing, including the date of their last day. This will help you to calculate any remaining annual leave and other benefits, and work out what their final pay will be. You should also ask them to set out their reasons for resignation. If this is because of any dispute or dissatisfaction with you or your company, you should let your lawyer know in case there is scope for a claim of 'constructive dismissal', where the employee feels they have no choice but to resign because of your actions.

- Announce the news to the rest of the team straight away.

- Begin organizing a handover process. It's amazing how quickly the time will pass, and suddenly years of knowledge of that particular job, including contacts, procedures, tricks of the trade, etc., are just walking out of the door. Work out what the person knows and the best way of transferring that knowledge to others in the company.

- On the last day you'll need to collect their office keys and any other company property. Then you should have all their computer passwords cancelled.

- You will need to provide them with a P45 form from HM Revenue and Customs.

Exit interviews

This is where you sit down for a chat with the person who is leaving and try to find out what lessons you can learn from their departure. This is particularly important if you wish that this person was staying. What went wrong? How can you avoid other people like them leaving? How can you make the company more attractive to people like them? You may have some specific questions to ask, but the most important thing is just to be there to listen and to ask prompting questions. A great technique is just to keep asking 'Why. . .?' to each answer, digging deeper into the reasons each time.

Do not try to argue with them about any of their views, or to justify any of your actions. The only way to get any value out of this exercise is to get the true picture of what they actually feel.

Alumni network

McKinsey are the world's leading management consultancy firm. They spend a lot of time and money recruiting the brightest people they can find in business. They then spend a lot of time and money training them.

Those people then leave after between five and ten years to pursue careers as entrepreneurs, chief executives, chief financial officers and so on at some of the world's leading companies.

Instead of being bitter and turning their back on these departing employees, McKinsey then spend a lot of time and money keeping in touch with them: organizing social events for former staff, keeping them in touch with company news, and so on.

Are they doing this purely because they like reunion parties? No. They're doing it because these people then become their customers. These people strongly believe that McKinsey are the best consultancy firm, because McKinsey hired them as a consultant, so they're perfectly prepared to hire McKinsey as long as there is no bitterness about their departure.

These ex-employees don't just become customers, they are also ambassadors, happily telling everyone in their new social and work circles about how great McKinsey are.

As you grow your company, people will leave. They will move away because of their partner changing jobs; they will need a job with more money because they're starting a family; they may have reached as high as they can in your company and need a new challenge. Whatever it is, don't take it too personally and don't shut them out. Do the exact opposite – help them always to feel a part of your company in some way:

- Have a 'Hall of Fame' showing all your current staff, but also with a section for former staff, including details on what they are doing now.

- Have events to which former staff are invited.

- Let them know they are welcome to visit.

- Ask them to keep in touch, and share their news around the company when you get it.

What else could you do to keep your former team members involved in the company in some way?

DISMISSAL OR REDUNDANCY

There's only one thing harder than a member of your team telling you they want to leave – and that's you having to tell a member of your team that you want them to leave.

If you're building your business successfully it will have a clear focus and a clear attitude. People will either 'get' this or they won't. People who are used to working in very big companies often won't understand what's expected of them in a smaller company. They won't understand the responsibilities that come with the freedoms. Their mindset will be focused on how to report their work to you so that it looks great, rather than actually on the work, their colleagues or their customers. They will seem great to you at first, but in a small company they can't hide their results in the same way they could in a big company, and the time may come to take the issue up with them.

There may also be other reasons why you would want someone to leave:

- Their attitude is poor and they are unprepared to change.

- Their skills are not up to scratch and they won't learn.

- They do not meet their responsibilities.

- They have done something seriously wrong (this may classify as gross misconduct).

- Their position has become redundant because of a change in the company's direction or poor sales.

Before dismissing anybody, you would normally work through a disciplinary procedure. This can include these steps:

1. Give them an informal oral warning. Tell them what your complaint about them is and what you would like them to do about it. Do this in private and make sure that you tell them that this warning is not part of the formal disciplinary procedure.

2. If the problem persists give them a formal written warning.

3. If the problem still persists give them a formal, written, final warning.

If these steps do not have the desired effect then you need to follow the statutory disciplinary and dismissal procedure:

1. Write to the team member, setting out your complaint and giving the date of a meeting to discuss the issue. They must be given plenty of time to prepare for this meeting and should be provided with copies of any evidence you intend to use against them. Make them aware that they may be accompanied to the meeting.

2. Hold the disciplinary meeting with the person concerned, setting out your complaint and evidence, and giving them the opportunity to respond and make their case.

3. Write to the team member after the meeting, setting out the decision you have made as a result of the meeting. Make them aware that they have the right to appeal against your decision.

4. If they decide to appeal, arrange a second meeting with them and seek further professional advice to guide you in the handling of this meeting.

You should always seek legal advice when instigating your disciplinary or dismissal procedure.

You can find further information at **www.acas.org.uk**.

HANDLING STAFF COMPLAINTS

Staff complaints, or 'grievances', must be handled in a particular way to comply with the legislation.

This is a three-step process:

1. The employee registers their complaint in writing. This should be given to their manager, or a more senior manager if the complaint involves their manager.

2. An appropriate manager then invites the employee to a meeting to investigate their complaint in detail and afterwards informs them of the outcome of the investigation into their complaint. The employee must be told of their right to appeal against this decision.

3. If the employee chooses to appeal a more senior manager (if possible) should invite them to a meeting to hear their appeal. After this meeting the employee should be informed of the final decision on their complaint.

Again, you can find further information at **www.acas.org.uk**.

RECORD-KEEPING

Your records for each member of staff must be kept for at least six years and should consist of:

● Their contact details.

● Contact details for next of kin.

● Notes from job interviews/application.

● Copy of employment contract.

● Copies of any official correspondence with them.

● Details of any disciplinary action.

● Payments made to them (required to ensure compliance with National Minimum Wage regulations).

● Hours worked (required to ensure compliance with Working Time regulations).

● Annual leave (required to ensure compliance with Working Time regulations).

● Time taken off sick (required if they have taken off more than four days).

● Details of any redundancy or termination meetings or correspondence (required to show compliance with employment law).

Be aware that under the Data Protection Act, you must:

● Have a reason for keeping any information about any staff member.

- Keep information secure and private.

- Show any member of staff any records you hold on them at their request.

You should also keep a general company record of:

- Any accidents, injuries and dangerous occurrences (where something happened that could have resulted in injury but didn't).

- Discussions with trade unions or employee representatives.

3

Managing the money

Financial management, including fulfilling obligations such as paying tax or filing accounts, is a real weak spot for many entrepreneurs.

I generally advise business owners to hire a bookkeeper for a day or two a month in the early days, perhaps taking someone on full time at a later stage in the growth of the business. This then frees up the time you, the entrepreneur, has to do what you're best at – finding customers and giving them what they want!

But you do need to know how to manage the money and understand what your obligations are as a business owner. This chapter will help you to do that.   .

INCOME

Invoicing

Some businesses, such as shops and restaurants, are lucky enough to be paid by their customers at the point-of-sale. If you can do this in your company it'll give a great boost to your finances, as you will often get paid by your customers before you have to pay your suppliers. The big super-markets have this advantage – they negotiate 90-day terms with their suppliers and sell the goods within days to their customers for cash or credit card payments which they will receive in cash a few days later. They then benefit from being able to invest a large portion of that cash for at least 80 days before having to pay it out to suppliers.

However, most businesses need to offer credit terms to their customers, particularly if the customers are other businesses. This means that when you deliver the goods or services to your customer, you present them with an invoice – setting out what you delivered, at what price and when that money needs to be paid by.

Tool

Invoice

An invoice is a request for payment from your customer and should include the following information:

1. The official company name. If you are operating as a sole trader or partnership, this is just your name(s). If you are operating as a limited company then you must show the full company name as registered at Companies House.

2. The trading name of the company. Sole traders sometimes use a company name other than simply their own name – for example, Fred Bloggs might trade as 'Speedy Cleaning', so he must show both names on the invoice. 'An Example Company Limited' might trade as 'Example Online', so again must show both names on the invoice.

3. The official address of the business. In the case of a limited company this would be the registered address. For a sole trader or partnership it can be any address where legal documents can be delivered to you.

4. If a limited company chooses to include the names of any directors on the invoice (as with any official stationery) then it must show the names of all directors.

5. A limited company must include the Company Registration Number.

6. The date on which the invoice was issued.

7. An invoice number. You do not have to start from number 1 if you are a start-up, but once you have started from a number you should use sequential numbers on invoices after that.

8. Your trading address for payment to be sent to, and perhaps a telephone number for your customer to contact you with any questions.

9. The name and address of the customer.

10. Details of the products or services you supplied the customer with. For example, '12 square oojamaflips, £10 each, £120'.

11. The total amount to be paid by the customer (see details below of how this needs to be split up if you are registered for VAT).

12. The payment terms you have agreed with the customer – for example, 'strictly 30 days net'.

13. A reference that the sale is subject to your standard Terms and Conditions of Sale (more information about these later).

14. If your company is registered for VAT then you must include the following:

    a) Your company's VAT registration number

    b) The date when the goods or services were provided to the customer

    c) The total amount of the invoice before VAT was added

    d) The total amount the customer needs to pay, including VAT.

There are sample Invoice templates on the CD-Rom.

It is good business practice to invoice for goods and services as quickly as possible after delivering them to the customer. The clock only starts ticking on the payment terms when the invoice is issued, so it's best to start that 30 days (or whatever your terms are) as soon as you can!

Insider Knowledge

A customer who has already bought from you once is the perfect prospect to sell to again. They know who you are, they know what you do and they obviously trust you enough to give you money. Therefore, don't just make your invoice a simple bill for money – make it a sales document. Include a promotion of another of your products or services.

In my companies we use a specially designed letterhead that is A4 in size, but with the main letter part a little narrower. We then use the space on the right hand side of the sheet for two tear-off coupons. Every time we send an invoice the top coupon contains a picture and some details of a product, while the bottom one is a simple order form – remember that you already know their contact details, so don't make them fill them in again, use a reference number.

If you just want to do something simple then enclose a separate flyer with an order form at the bottom – but make sure you try to sell more to existing customers, every time you contact them, even on your invoices!

Accepting payments

When the credit term you have granted to your customer is over you will (hopefully) get paid. If not, see the 'Debt collection' section below.

There is a range of ways you can choose to accept payments.

Cash

This is how many retailers of smaller items get paid, but it's rarely used in business to business transactions. When customers pay by cash it's well worth having a device to check that notes are not forged. These devices are available from cash and carry stores or business supply catalogues. If a customer wants to pay you a large amount in cash, when other customers normally pay you by other methods, then it's worth being suspicious. Do you know the customer? Can you check the notes are genuine?

Cheques

These are less frequently used by retail customers who now mostly pay by credit card, but cheques are still widely used by businesses to pay for purchases. It is better for you if you can persuade your customers to pay electronically (see below) as banks charge more money for processing cheques.

Electronic payments

This is a rapidly growing method of payment between businesses. The higher level of electronic payment is known as 'BACS', but different banks have simpler, cheaper systems for smaller businesses that are often known as 'Electronic Bill Payments' or similar. Nearly all business bank accounts can receive this type of payment, and you will often pay only about 30 per cent of the processing fee normally applied to receiving cheque payments.

Credit cards

In many industries customers now expect to be able to pay by credit card, and this is also becoming the case even with business to business sales, as companies begin using company credit cards or corporate purchasing cards.

This can be an expensive way of accepting payments but there are many benefits too:

- Customers consider it to be very convenient.

- It can increase sales as customers who don't have other payment methods to hand make impulse purchases.

- Foreign customers can easily buy from you with the card company handling the currency exchange.

- Cards are less open to fraud or rejected payments than cheques

If you want to accept credit or debit card payments in your business you will need to set up a 'merchant account'.

Insider Knowledge

A 'merchant account' is a service provided by a bank that allows you to accept payments from credit or debit cards. You are provided with a Card Payment Terminal (which needs to be connected to a phone line), or with an online virtual terminal facility to process cards. Each day this terminal communicates with the bank and tells it about the day's transactions. The bank then collects that money from the cardholder's bank, holds on to it for a bit (don't they always?) and then pays it into your normal business bank account.

The bank charges you a monthly fee (usually around £20) plus a percentage of any transactions processed (usually in the region of 2 per cent to 5 per cent depending on the volume of transactions). Debit card transactions are charged as a fixed fee rather than a percentage.

Standard merchant accounts will allow you to process Visa, Mastercard, Maestro (formerly Switch) and Solo. To accept other card types you will need to set up a separate account with that card provider.

To open a merchant account you can use any one of the main high street banks or an online provider such as WorldPay. They will want to get a lot of information from you to ensure you are financially sound and low risk to them. They will want to know about the products and services you provide, the total value of monthly sales you expect to make via credit card, the average value per transaction and some details about your business history and performance. Start-up businesses can find it difficult to open merchant services accounts. If you are turned down by one provider, it is worth trying others as they do have different criteria.

At first the bank will insist on charging you at the high end of the scale – that is, around 5 per cent per credit card transaction or 40p per debit card transaction. However, you can negotiate this down quite a lot after about six months, and then further every six months after that, once they can see that you are generating sufficient sales volumes and have a low level of fraud occurring in your payments.

Insider Knowledge

I have found merchant services providers to be universally awful – and every entrepreneur I know seems to think the same. They are awkward and unhelpful when you want to open an account, they are unhelpful when you want to check on particular card transactions, they keep making mistakes, they seem to charge a lot of money, and they seem to be slow to pass the customer's money on to you. But being able to take credit card payments can be essential for many businesses, so we entrepreneurs have little choice!

If you do accept credit card transactions there are some things you can do to minimize fraud:

1. Get the customer's card billing address at the time of purchase (this won't always be practical for smaller value retail sales).

2. Get a customer telephone number.

3. Check the customer's signature carefully – and train your staff to do the same. It's amazing how often people don't even glance at my signature when I pay for things.

4. Change your card processing equipment to accept Chip and PIN cards as soon as possible, as this gives much greater security. If you receive a correct PIN (which will be confirmed at the time of the transaction) then you are not liable for any fraudulent transactions.

5. If you accept card payments online then sign up to use one of the anti-fraud schemes such as 'Verified by Visa' or 'Mastercard Securecode'.

6. If you accept payments online or over the phone (known as 'Customer Not Present' transactions or 'CNP') then ask for the last three digits on the back of the card's signature strip as a further security precaution.

7. Merchant account providers will often offer address verification services for CNP transactions, allowing you to check that the card is registered at the address you have been given.

Credit control

Invoicing is only a request for payment – it does not ensure that you actually do get paid. To make sure that you only grant credit to creditworthy companies and that they do pay on time, there are a number of steps that you can take.

Account applications

Whenever a customer asks for credit terms (i.e. they want to be invoiced for the goods and then pay you at a later date), you should have them fill in an Account Application form.

This form gives you important information about their business and allows you to take some steps to protect yourself against non-payment of your invoices, or even fraudulent transactions.

A template Account Application form is included on the CD-Rom.

Once the customer returns this form to you, you can use the details provided to do the following checks:

1. Run a credit check with one of the credit reference agencies (see **www.equifax.co.uk**, **www.experian.co.uk** or **www.dnb.com/uk**).

2. Write to the trade references the customer has given and ask them to provide a reference. Make it easy for them by providing a standard form (a sample form is included on the CD-Rom) that they can fill in very quickly and return in a stamped addressed envelope provided by you.

3. Obtain a reference from the customer's bank. You will need to get them to fill in a consent form for this and send it on to the bank with your request. This is only worth doing for higher value sales and in conjunction with other checks. The bank will charge you for providing a reference.

4. Seek views on the customer from people you know who may know them.

5. For very high value sales, or if it's easy to do anyway, it's worth having your sales person visit the customer's premises and report

back. They should talk to as many of the customer's staff as they can and look for any signs as to how well the business is doing.

If all these checks show that the customer is creditworthy then you can open an account for them and set a credit limit. This limit is the maximum amount of money that they can owe you at any one time. If they reach this limit and place another order then they have to pay off some of their debt to you before you will process the new order, ensuring that they don't go over this limit. You can start a customer on a low credit limit, but increase it over time as they demonstrate their ability to pay.

Insider Knowledge

When using trade references in your credit checks do bear in mind that the customer will only have provided you with referees who will give good references. So don't rely entirely on these, but use the information together with the others to build up a rounded picture.

Terms and Conditions of Sale

For every customer, whether or not they pay on account, you should have a set of standard Terms and Conditions of Sale that they agree to in advance of you delivering the goods or services.

Tool

Terms and Conditions of Sale

Your Terms and Conditions of Sale are an important legal document and should be drawn up, or at least checked, by your lawyer. They can significantly help you in claiming money owed to you or avoiding arguments over orders.

In general they will set out the following:

1. What the price of the goods will be and whether this price includes shipping, taxes or other charges.

2. What the payment terms for orders will be.

3. How and when the goods will be delivered.

4. Who will own the goods at each stage and who will own the risk in the goods at each stage. Generally, the risk passes to the buyer when they take delivery, but the ownership (known as 'Title') of the goods does not pass to the buyer until they have paid in full.

5. What will happen if the customer wants to cancel an order.

6. What will happen if you fail to deliver the goods or services.

7. What will happen if the goods or services are faulty or substandard.

8. What will happen if the customer fails to pay in full and on time.

You will find a Terms and Conditions of Sale template on the CD-Rom.

In the context of this chapter, the important part of your terms and conditions relates to the payment terms, and to what will happen if payment is not made on time.

Payment terms are the time a customer has to pay an invoice. There are a number of commonly used terms:

- **Net x days** – where 'x' is the number of days (not just working days) that a customer has to pay following the date of an invoice. While 7, 14, 30, 60 and 90 are all common here, 30 is the most common.

- **End of Month** – This means that all invoices raised in the month must be settled by the end of the same month.

- **End of Month following Invoice** – this means that the invoice is payable at the end of the month after the month it was raised.

- **30 days month end** – mostly the same as the option above, but it means that the invoice is payable at the end of the month in which it has aged by 30 days.

- **14th of the Month following Invoice** – invoices are to be settled on the 14th of the calendar month after the month in which the invoice was raised.

- **Cash on Delivery** – payment (by any method, not actually by cash) must be made when the customer takes delivery of the goods.

The most common terms to use are Net x days.

You may also choose to insist that a customer makes an advance payment of a certain amount before the work begins. This is often expressed as a percentage, such as 30 per cent or 50 per cent advance payment. It is highly advisable to take an advance payment or deposit if the work you will carry out for the customer is highly customized or specialized, and if it will be difficult to sell to someone else if they renege on the deal.

Some companies have a system of staged payments, with a part payment with the order, part payment at certain milestones in the work and the remaining payment on completion.

There may be standard payment terms for your industry that you will want to consider. Don't rule out trying something different, but better payment terms can be a competitive advantage to some customers, so you may find it difficult to impose tougher payment terms than your competitors.

You may want to offer a discount for early payment of your invoices. So your standard terms might be Net 30 days, but you could offer a discount if customers pay within seven days (or any period you like, but do be aware of the financial cost of this to your business; it can also be difficult to phase out these discounts once they have become the standard). However, this can encourage customers with good cash flow to take advantage of the offer to get a better price, and give you the benefit of better cash flow. This can be very difficult to police however, with some cheeky customers still taking the discount even though they don't pay in the shorter time.

If a customer doesn't pay on time you can charge interest, which you should set out in your Terms and Conditions of Sale, even though you are automatically given this right by law. You are allowed to charge interest at 8 per cent over the Bank of England's base rate.

Confirmation of order

Whenever you receive an order from a customer, send them a written confirmation of the order, including all the agreed details relating to price, date of delivery, specifications and so on. This can avoid problems at a later stage and gives you a much better position if a dispute does arise.

Enclose a copy of your standard Terms and Conditions of Sale with every order confirmation, stating on the order confirmation that it is subject to these terms.

Confirmation of delivery

When you provide your service, or deliver a product, to your customer be sure to get them to sign a confirmation. This might be a courier's delivery note or a 'Work Completion Confirmation' that you have drawn up yourself.

In effect, the document will say that they have received the goods and services they had ordered, and that they are in good condition or they are satisfied with the work carried out.

Some service businesses get customers to sign such documents at key milestones in the project, or even after each day or week's work. This helps you because it forces the customer to raise any problems at an early stage so you can resolve them, or it gives you documentary evidence that will lend strong support to your claim for money in court if the customer later tries to avoid paying.

Debt collection

If a customer still fails to pay your invoice on time then you can take a number of steps to recover the money – the first of which is actually worth doing even before the money is due. These steps are a guideline and can be varied depending on your relationship with the customer or the frequency of their orders.

1. Send a statement of account before the invoice becomes due, or on a monthly basis for regular customers.

2. Send a letter on the day after the invoice becomes due, saying the money is now overdue and payment should be made immediately – but please ignore this letter if payment has already been made.

3. Phone your customer contact, or the accounts department, a few days later if payment has still not been received. Remind them of the terms and conditions of sale that they have agreed to. Get an answer as to when payment will be made. Ask them if there is a problem with the product or service, or with their finances.

4. Write another, more formal and serious letter requesting immediate payment.

5. Suspend delivery of any further goods or services to the customer.

6. Contact your customer on the phone or in person and try to find an amicable way to resolve the problem. Perhaps agree a repayment schedule to help them out if they are normally good customers. Consider insisting on 'Cash on Delivery' terms for orders until the account is back in order.

7. At this stage you may like to consider passing the matter to a debt collection agency or to your solicitor. A debt collection agency may charge up to 10 per cent of the amount they reclaim from your customer.

8. You may also choose to pursue the matter through the courts. Send a letter to the customer saying that if payment is not received by a certain date you will begin legal proceedings. You can initiate the proceedings by using the excellent online service provided by the government's Court Service. Visit **www.moneyclaim.gov.uk**, or you can get the forms to make a claim on paper by visiting or telephoning your local county court.

Options 7 and 8 may mean that the relationship with the customer breaks down completely and they won't deal with you again – but then you might not want to deal with them again either! Do try to resolve matters amicably first, as this is also the cheaper option. As soon as solicitors get involved you can wave goodbye to large chunks of cash!

If you do decide to take further action then you need to take account of the amount outstanding and the debtor's ability to pay. You might spend a lot of time and money chasing what is actually a relatively small amount that you stand little chance of getting.

If you already have a firm of solicitors who work with you on a regular basis then they can probably provide quite a cost-effective service to help existing clients pursue bad debts, but if you go cold to a firm of solicitors who you have not dealt with before it may end up being a costly exercise.

For more information to help you get customer payments on time, and what to do if you don't, see **www.payontime.co.uk**.

EXPENDITURE

Paying staff

Depending on your industry, and the types of workers you employ, you may be expected to pay wages weekly or monthly. This is up to you and your staff to decide.

It's becoming increasingly standard to pay the money straight into employees' bank accounts using BACS or other electronic transfer payments. In some cases cheques, or even cash, are still used, however. If you do pay in cash then give careful consideration to security issues on pay days.

The method you use is up to you, but it's worth bearing in mind your employees' preferences (as a group – you can't be expected to pay everyone in different ways!) and setting out or agreeing the method of payment when you recruit new staff.

There are a couple of factors you need to consider in relation to paying your staff:

1. National Minimum Wage. This is a minimum rate of pay per hour's work that is required by law in the UK. When calculating whether you meet this minimum you can take into account commissions and other performance related incentives and bonuses, as well as any tips that your staff receive through the payroll. Employee benefits, overtime or shift-work premiums don't count.

2. You must provide four weeks' paid annual leave for your staff. This can be pro-rata for part-time staff.

Other than that, the amount you pay your staff for the work they do is up to you – and of course them! If they don't like the rate of pay they'll go elsewhere. Also, you may have heard of performance related pay, but if you don't pay very well you'll get the opposite – pay related performance.

Some companies choose to pay at or slightly below the market rate for a job, but to make the job tremendously exciting, stimulating and rewarding in other ways. That way they know they are attracting people who aren't just in it for the money, but who are passionate about what they do. But that only works in some industries and some companies.

Other companies choose to pay above the average market rate, in order to be able to recruit above average staff. If you choose to do this then make sure your recruitment process is robust so that you're recruiting staff who are genuinely above average at the job, not just above average at giving job interviews.

You should have a feel for what the industry average pay is for the kind of jobs in your company, both through your own experience and the research you have done in your market. But for further research get a few papers with job sections, look in your trade press, and look at online recruitment websites, in order to get an idea of what pay is expected in return for what work.

Additionally, the government uses companies' payroll systems to administer the payments of a number of benefits. As a result, you must:

1. Pay Statutory Maternity Pay to employees who are on maternity leave, but you can reclaim these payments through the PAYE and National Insurance Contributions you make to HM Revenue and Customs.

2. Pay Statutory Paternity Pay and Statutory Adoption Pay.

3. Pay Statutory Sick Pay to employees who are unable to work for four days or more due to illness. Statutory Sick Pay is payable for up to 28 weeks for any one period of sickness.

4. Collect repayments of student loans from employees through deductions from their wages. You only need to do this if you receive a Start Notice from HM Revenue and Customs. It's up to them to know which of your employees this applies to and to tell you to make the deductions.

5. Pay the Working Tax Credit. You pay this to employees who meet the criteria by adding it to their wage slip, and then deducting the amount from what you would normally have paid to HM Revenue and Customs via the PAYE scheme. Seek advice from your accountant or from HM Revenue and Customs if you are asked to make these payments.

For more information on PAYE and National Insurance, see those sections later in this chapter.

Finally, however and whatever you pay your staff you must provide them with a pay statement (pay slip). This must show the total amount they earned (gross pay), an itemized list of any deductions that were made (PAYE, NI, etc.) and then the final amount that will actually be paid to them (net pay). If they receive any tax credits then these must also be shown separately.

Paying suppliers

In the same way that you have set out our Terms and Conditions of Sale, including payment terms, to your customers, your suppliers will have similar documents. Make sure you know what each supplier has stipulated so that you don't end up in a dispute with them, interrupting the supply of goods or services to your business.

While you shouldn't pay early unless a discount is offered, you shouldn't pay late either. I know it's heartbreaking to write out those big cheques and send them off, but someone out there needs to receive that cheque just as much as you need to receive the payments from your customers.

However, if you do end up with a cash flow problem – a temporary one – then your suppliers may be prepared to help, particularly if you've always paid on time in the past. If it's just going to be a week late they probably won't worry too much, but for any more than that, get in touch with them to explain the situation and to indicate when it will be resolved. Reasonable people will often be only too happy to help. Remember though that it is much better to ask first than just to keep quiet and hope they don't notice.

Most companies these days prefer to be paid by BACS or other electronic payment, and this is best for you too as your bank will charge you less for each payment made. However, you will get some who see electronic payments as some kind of weird hi-tech thing and prefer to receive a paper cheque through the post even though it takes longer and costs them more.

Like we discussed above, some payment terms can include a discount for early payment. If your supplier offers this to you, is it worth taking? The first thing to check is your cash flow forecast – would paying the money early cause you any problems? If not, the next stage is to see what the value is to you. You can do that by using the following calculation:

Percentage discount x (365/number of days you'd have to pay in without the discount)

This puts the discount on an annual basis so that you can compare it to the annual interest rate you earn on money in your bank account.
So, for example, you owe a customer £10,000 on 30-day terms. He offers you a 2.5 per cent discount for immediate payment. That means the calculation looks like this:

2.5% x (365/30) = 30.4%

Now, compare the figure of 30.4 per cent with the interest that your bank will pay you on money that sits in your account. You'll find that a generous bank will typically pay 0.1 per cent interest on money in your current account, but some current accounts don't pay any interest at all! A savings account might earn between 1 per cent and 3 per cent interest. This means that you get a much better benefit from using the money to pay your supplier early than by hanging onto it.

Paying your accountant

It's well worth agreeing a fee with your accountant for everything that you will need them to do for you over the year, such as the annual accounts, Corporation Tax return, Annual Return and so on. Then pay them one-twelfth of this by standing order each month. This helps to avoid a big surprise fee at the end of the year.

For any additional work you ask your accountant, or other advisers, to do you should insist on receiving a quotation which you have to approve before they begin the work.

Accountants charge by the hour for any work by themselves or their staff, and fees can vary wildly, but are generally dependent on the size of the firm. If it's one of the national or international firms, you can generally forget about hiring them in a small entrepreneurial business as hourly fees for partners will be into three figures. Fees for a partner in a more regional firm could be between £50 and £90 an hour, while fees for a more local firm might be between £30 and £60 per hour.

To get the best rate from your accountant, ensure that you present your records to them in an orderly way. You may not believe it but some people do just dump all their receipts and invoices for the year in a box and hand them over. Once, when I was at my accountants, a guy came in and dumped a suitcase at reception. The thing was crammed full with disorganized papers, and the accountant's face just dropped – a facial expression that is directly opposite to the direction of the fee.

Accountants can specialize in different areas, so search for one that knows about your type or size of business. When you meet them, ask them about other clients they have that are similar to you (though they won't be able to give you names, they can talk in general terms).

In general though, the relationship with your accountant will be one of the most important relationships with someone external to your company. They can provide you with valuable advice, careful planning and a bit of experience. And you'll hopefully be working with them for years. It's well worth shopping around to find an accountant that you like and know you can work with.

Of course, the same accountant may not be right for your business for ever. As you grow you may need to move to a practice that has more experience of the issues faced by larger businesses, and you will need to do the same shopping around exercise then.

TAXATION

This is the subject that makes so many people visibly wince – taking your hard earned money and paying it to the government. Well, you have no choice in the matter so I suggest two things: first, get an accountant or bookkeeper to sort it out for you and save you a lot of time and hassle; and second, think of what you are buying with your taxes rather than seeing it as money down the drain. I think the government is very poor at explaining what we get in return for our taxes, focusing instead on telling us we have no choice but to pay them.

Your taxes pay for:

● The roads you, your team and your products travel to customers on.

● The education you received (everybody receives some input from government finances into their education at some stage).

● The education your employees received, and your future employees are receiving now.

● Healthcare for you and your staff.

● Many other things large and small.

Okay, lecture over, but you get my point – let's look at the benefits rather than just moaning about having to pay. And if you still don't like the taxation system then run for public office and be the one to change it!

Entrepreneurs should be proud of the immense contribution they make to society by earning money both for themselves and for the nation through the taxes they pay and the jobs they create. But don't get carried away, just be sure to pay the minimum amount of tax you have to pay by law and be proud of it.

PAYE

This stands for Pay As You Earn, and is the deduction of Income Tax and National Insurance Contributions from employees' pay by their employer. It is the obligation of all employers to calculate any Income Tax and National Insurance Contributions from the amounts you pay your staff. It is administered by HM Revenue and Customs (HMRC), which was formerly the Inland Revenue.

You need to make these calculations monthly (or quarterly if the average monthly total is likely to be less than £1,500), and then send the amounts deducted to HM Revenue and Customs by the 19th of the following month (or the 22nd if you pay by electronic transfer).

I highly recommend using your accountant, a bookkeeper or a payroll bureau to manage your payroll for you, as PAYE can be complicated and time consuming – you are far better focusing your attention on your sales and customers. If you really do want to do your payroll yourself then my next recommendation is to use a computer software package to do it. The main accountancy packages are Sage, Quickbooks and Mamut.

If you are starting a new business you need to contact HMRC New Employers Helpline on 0845 60 70 143 and ask for a Starter Pack and a PAYE reference number.

If you run an existing business then you can get help from the HMRC Employers Helpline on 08457 143 143, or you can order advice booklets and the standard forms by calling the HMRC Employers Orderline on 08457 646 646. You can also find any information you need at their website: **www.hmrc.gov.uk.**

Tool

Income Tax

You need to deduct Income Tax from the pay of all members of staff who earn above the PAYE threshold of £94 a week or £408 a month (check for the latest figures).

You need a tax code for each employee. They should be able to give you a P45 form, given to them from the last job they left. If they do not have this you will need to use an emergency tax code temporarily and get them to fill in a form P46 which you will then return to HMRC.

Using this tax code, in combination with the Tax Tables you will be provided with by HMRC, you can then fill in form P11 (the

Deductions Working Sheet) each month to work out the deductions you need to make from the pay of each employee.

As well as the money paid in salary, you and your staff will be taxed on 'benefits in kind', such as company cars, health insurance and gym membership.

Tool

National Insurance Contributions

You need to deduct National Insurance Contributions (NICs) from any earnings over the National Insurance earnings threshold from all members of staff who are aged 16 or over.

Employers pay Class 1 contributions on behalf of their employees (having deducted the amounts from wages), and additional payments as the employer's contribution is based on wages paid and benefits in kind. If your business is a limited company then be aware that you must also pay Class 1 NICs on any pay that company directors receive, but that this is calculated differently to Class 1 contributions on pay to normal employees. Your bookkeeper or accountant can advise you.

If you are running your business as a sole trader or partnership then you pay Class 2 and Class 4 NICs.

You calculate NICs using the same P11 form as you do for Income Tax.

You can pay your tax electronically (earning you some extra time and some financial benefits), or you can pay by cheque or cash by using pay slips provided by HMRC (P30B for individual pay slips, or P30BC for a pay slip booklet). Use form P32 to keep a record of the payments that you make each month.

Following the end of each tax year (5 April), you need to fill in a P14 End of Year Summary form for each employee, summarizing all the payments you have made to them and the deductions of tax and NICs from those payments. You then give each employee a copy of this information using a form P60. At the same time you will need to complete an employer's annual return (form P35) and return this to HMRC.

You also need to fill in a P11D form for all staff, including directors (if your business is a limited company) at the end of the tax year. This gives details of any taxable benefits they have received, such as company cars or health insurance. Certain benefits are not taxable, such as free or subsidized meals at work, drinks or refreshments at work, mobile phones or relocation expenses.

When staff leave your company you'll need to fill in a form P45, giving the form to your employee for them to take to their next job.

As you can see, administering PAYE is quite involved, with many forms to complete and calculations to perform. I strongly advise using your accountant, bookkeeper or a payroll bureau to administer it for you, or use a computer software package if you insist on doing it yourself.

VAT

VAT stands for Value Added Tax, and is a form of taxation known in many countries as Sales Tax. The idea is that companies charge their customers a tax on each order, which is a percentage of the value of the sale.

So why is it called Value Added Tax? Simply because you only end up paying tax on the value that your company adds to a particular product or service – the difference between the price you sell it at and the price you bought it at.

Let's look at an example for VAT in which you plan to sell 'Fruit Smoothie Kits'.

1. You buy food blenders from an electrical wholesaler for a 40 per cent discount on the Recommended Retail Price of £29.78 + VAT, so you pay £17.87 + VAT. Therefore, the VAT you pay your supplier on this transaction is £3.13 per blender (at a VAT rate of 17.5 per cent).

2. You have fruit smoothie drinks recipe cards designed and printed by a local printer who charges you £400 + VAT for 100 copies of ten different cards. You pay £70 of VAT on this transaction. Each pack of ten cards costs you £4, and you have paid 70p of VAT on each pack (at a rate of 17.5 per cent).

3. You buy pairs of drinking glasses with a cool design and built-in spiral drinking straw from a local catering wholesaler for £1 per pair plus VAT of 17.5p (again, at a rate of 17.5 per cent).

To purchase the materials for each kit has therefore cost you £22.87 plus VAT of £4. You decide you can sell these kits for £55 each, inclusive of VAT, to your customers. That means you are effectively charging £46.81 plus £8.19 of VAT.

Let's assume, to make the illustration easier, that you have actually only bought enough materials for one kit and that you have sold that one kit. So, when the time comes to fill in your VAT return for the period, you have made VAT-able purchases of £22.87, and VAT-able sales of £46.81. The value you have added is therefore £23.94, and this is the amount you pay tax on – the 'Value Added'.

On the VAT form this amount is arrived at by declaring to HMRC the £8.19 of VAT you have collected from your customer (known as 'output tax'), and reclaiming the £4 of VAT you have paid to your suppliers (known as 'input tax'). You then only pay the difference of £4.19 to HMRC.

Registering for VAT

All businesses with an annual turnover greater than a certain amount (currently £60,000, but do check for the most up to date figure) must register for VAT, but there are also advantages to some businesses of registering voluntarily. Your accountant or bookkeeper will be able to advise you whether voluntary registration is worthwhile.

HMRC is actually very helpful, and if you have any questions about VAT it's well worth calling their helpline on 0845 010 9000.

Insider Knowledge

When you first register for VAT you can claim back the VAT on any goods that you bought in the last three years as long as you still own them and they were supplied for use in your business. You can reclaim VAT on any services you paid for in the last six months as long as they were provided to you for your business. In each case you must have an invoice or receipt that clearly identifies the goods or services, the date they were supplied, their cost, the VAT charged and the VAT number of the seller.

As well as the standard way of accounting for VAT, HMRC has introduced a number of alternative schemes to make VAT more user friendly for certain businesses, particularly smaller companies.

Cash Accounting

This differs from the standard scheme, in that you pay VAT on actual *payments* you make and receive, rather than when you send out invoices or receive bills.

Most business with a turnover under £660,000 can choose this scheme.

This scheme will benefit your cash flow if your customers take some time to pay your invoices (e.g. 60 days), but you have to pay your suppliers quite quickly (e.g. 14 days).

Annual accounting

Under the standard scheme you have to fill in a return every quarter, but under this scheme that is reduced to once a year. Instead, HMRC estimate what you are likely to pay per year, and divide this into nine interim payments and a final balancing payment at the end of the year when you fill in your VAT return.

You can select this scheme if your VAT-able turnover is likely to be less than £150,000 per annum. However, if you have already been VAT registered for more than 12 months you can select to move on to this scheme as long as your annual VAT-able turnover is less than £660,000.

Flat rate scheme

Under this scheme HMRC gives you a flat rate percentage of VAT to pay them on all sales you make, based on the industry you are in.

So, for example, an IT consultant would pay a flat rate of 13 per cent.

The idea is that this saves you a whole load of paperwork – you don't need to keep records of the VAT on each sale or purchase, you don't need to keep lots of VAT receipts for items you buy and you don't have to do any more than one calculation to fill in your VAT return.

HMRC has estimated what proportion of VAT-able expenses you will have to reclaim the VAT on, based on averages in your industry. They have then simply reduced the 17.5 per cent standard VAT rate you pay to take account of this.

You would still charge your customers the standard VAT rate of 17.5 per cent of each sale, but you would only pay 13 per cent (in this case) of the value of each sale to HMRC – the difference is what allows for the expenses you would normally have reclaimed.

This can save you a lot of time as you don't need to keep as many records and you don't need to worry about what expenses you are allowed to claim back and what you're not.

Businesses with a VAT-able turnover of less than £150,000 per annum, and a total sales turnover of less than £187,500, can select this scheme – but there are some other conditions you need to meet. Ask HMRC for details.

Retail schemes

There are a number of schemes intended for use by shops and other businesses that deal with a large number of customers making transactions of relatively small value and that can't reasonably be expected to be providing full VAT invoices for each one. However, you do still have to provide a VAT invoice if a customer asks for one.

These schemes are more involved and you will need to seek advice from your accountant or HMRC on whether you qualify to use one of them, and whether it would benefit you.

Charging VAT

Once your company is registered for VAT, you need to charge the tax on any sales you make and highlight that any prices in quotations you give are subject to VAT.

Some products or services are exempt from VAT (HMRC or your advisers can tell you if you fall into this category), but if VAT applies to what you sell it may be charged at one of three rates:

- **Standard Rate.** This is currently 17.5 per cent and applies to most goods or services.

- **Reduced Rate.** This is currently 5 per cent and applies to a few goods and services such as provision of gas or electricity.

- **Zero Rate.** This is, unsurprisingly, zero per cent and applies to a few goods and services such as books.

Businesses that sell directly to individual consumers often include VAT in the price they quote, so they will display the price as £14.99, but it is actually £12.76 plus VAT.

Businesses that sell to other businesses tend to exclude VAT from the prices they quote, as their customers can normally reclaim it so don't see it as part of the real cost of the product. Thus they will quote their prices as £99 plus VAT, for example.

Claiming back VAT

Once you register for VAT you need to obtain VAT invoices or receipts for anything you buy that VAT is charged on. This includes general expenses, such as petrol, some travel expenses, hotel accommodation and so on, as well as the normal costs of doing what your business does.

Any VAT invoice or receipt you are given must include:

- Details of the product or service supplied.

- The quantity of products supplied.

- The unit price.

- The VAT rate applicable.

- The total amount of the sale excluding VAT.

- The total amount of the sale including VAT.

- The selling company's name.

- The selling company's address.

- The selling company's VAT registration number.

- Preferably your company's name and address.

Filling in your VAT return

For most businesses this is done on a quarterly basis, with the quarters normally set up to fit into your trading year if you are running a limited company.

Your VAT return must be filed within one month of the end of each of these quarters. A few weeks before this, you will receive the form through the post.

Don't be frightened when awaiting your first VAT return, as it's actually really simple to fill in – it's just nine boxes to complete and a space for your name and signature, and it's all on one side of A4! Once again, the staff at HMRC's VAT helpline are very friendly and helpful and will be able to answer your questions.

You can also fill in your VAT return online (you can register for this service via HMRC's website).

If you use computer accounts software then all the main packages are able to provide you with the details you need for your VAT return at the click of a button – and some can even print it for you!

Corporation Tax

This is a tax paid only by limited companies, clubs and societies, co-operatives and certain other legal corporate entities – but not by self-employed people, so if you're a sole trader or in a partnership you can skip this section.

When you form your business you need to fill in form CT41G to tell HMRC about your company.

Then you must file your Corporation Tax return (form CT600) within 12 months of your year-end. However, you must pay the actual tax within nine months (and one day, but that's just getting picky) of your financial-year end.

Corporation Tax is a tax on the profits you make in the year, but there are extra charges or allowances (discounts) on items you sell or purchase during the year.

The tax is charged at the following rates (current at the time of publication, but do check for updates with HMRC or your accountant):

- **Starting Rate.** This is 0 per cent on profits of up to £10,000 that are retained in the business, or 19 per cent for profits that are distributed to shareholders.

- **Small Companies Rate.** This is 19 per cent for profits between £50,001 and £300,000.

- **Main Rate.** This is 30 per cent for profits over £1.5m.

If your profits fall in between these rates then the rate gradually steps up, under something known as 'Marginal Relief' in order not to penalize companies with profits that just tip over into a higher rate. Your accountant will calculate your corporation tax as part of doing your annual accounts.

Income Tax Self Assessment

Income Tax on the profits of the business is only paid by people who are self-employed (i.e. sole traders or partnerships) and is instead of Corporation Tax. If you are in this category you will need to fill in a Self Assessment form each year.

However, directors of limited companies must also fill in an Income Tax Self Assessment form, even if no other tax is payable on top of the PAYE that has already been deducted by the company from the directors' salary.

The Self Assessment form is known as the SA100 and will usually be sent to you automatically if you need to fill one in, but if you don't receive one (normally in April) then contact HMRC's Self Assessment Orderline on 0845 9000 404.

Sole traders will also need to fill in an additional sheet SA103, while Partners in a partnership will need to fill out SA104. You will also need to pay a first payment on account by 31 January during the current tax year, and this is usually equivalent to half of the tax you paid last year. Then you need to make a second payment on account by 31 July following the end of the tax year. Finally, a balancing payment or refund is made by 31 January in the following year.

Employees and company directors will need to fill in SA101. Your tax needs to be paid by the 31 January in the year following the end of the tax year in question.

If you fill in the form, and want HMRC to work out the tax you owe, you must send the forms back to them by 30 September following the end of the tax year in question (which always ends on 5 April). Otherwise it must reach HMRC no later than 31 January in the following year. But don't leave it until the last minute if you don't have to!

If you need any help, ask your accountant or call the Self Assessment Helpline on 0845 9000 444.

Business Rates

These are the business equivalent of Council Tax and are payable to your local authority to fund local services. They are charged on the premises that you use to carry out your business and can even include part of your home if you work from there.

You normally receive the rates bill in March or April, and then pay in ten monthly instalments after that.

The rateable value of your premises is set by the Valuation Office Agency. You can contact their helpline on 0845 602 1507 if you have any questions about the value given to your property.

There have been a number of cases where businesses have successfully appealed against the valuation placed on their premises and have had their Business Rates reduced as a result. A chartered surveyor can help you with such an appeal, and you can contact the Royal Institution of Chartered Surveyors on 0870 333 1600.

INSURANCE

You should consult an insurance broker for more information on insurance or to arrange a policy. It is important to select a broker that is authorized by the Financial Services Authority. You can search for brokers in your area at the website of the Institute of Insurance Brokers, at **www.iib-uk.com**.

The following are the most common insurance policies that small businesses need.

Premises

If you rent or lease your premises then the landlord will normally be responsible for arranging suitable insurance for the building, but you should check your agreement with them or ask them directly. If you run a shop you may be responsible for insuring the façade, including the window (for which a separate Glass Insurance policy is often available), while the landlord is responsible for insuring the rest of the fabric of the building. This sort of insurance isn't compulsory by law but may be required in your lease.

Contents

This insurance covers anything within your premises that isn't part of the fabric of the building itself – for example, stock, computers, machinery and furniture.

You can opt for a policy that will pay out for a brand new replacement of any items you claim for, or you can get a cheaper policy that will pay out the current value of the items you claim for.

This insurance isn't required by law, but it is a very sensible move.

Employer's liability

This insurance is compulsory for any company employing people other than the owner.

If an employee is injured at work your business could be liable for great expense. The statutory minimum cover is £5m but the normal level offered by insurers is £10m.

It is a statutory requirement to retain all employer's liability insurance certificates for 40 years (in case a former employee makes a claim for an injury or illness caused in the past). The Health and Safety Executive (HSE) enforces the law on employer's liability insurance and can issue fines of up to £2,500 for any day a business does not hold suitable cover.

Public liability

You must have this insurance if any members of the public will visit your premises, or if you will do things where there are members of the public. There are very few people whose businesses don't fall into these categories!

You'll need it if you run a shop, restaurant, hotel or other place where your customers visit. You'll need it if you organize events, carry out work at a client's premises or anything else where you take your products or services into a public place.

The risks are that a member of the public might be injured or killed by something you and your staff do, or forget to do. They might trip over a cable, get food poisoning, slip on a wet surface and so on.

Key man

This is a general term for insurance policies that help protect the company against the loss of people who are key to the running of the business.

This starts with life insurance, which pays out if the person dies, but you can add critical illness cover to this as an option, which will pay out if they are unable to work because of one of a list of serious illnesses, or even if they are able to work but are diagnosed with a very serious illness.

You can arrange group policies to get better prices on life and critical illness policies for all your key staff.

Motor

If your company operates any vehicles, or provides company cars to staff, you must ensure that they are insured. The level of cover must be appropriate for the use of the vehicle, with travelling sales people being among the most expensive to cover (and you'll understand why if you've ever seen them drive their BMWs on the motorway!). This is an absolute legal requirement.

But your responsibility does not stop there. If you or any of your staff use a personally owned vehicle for travelling on business (not including commuting to or from work), you must ensure that the personal motor insurance policy that you, or they, have is extended to cover this use.

For vehicles that your company insures, you will find that the insurer places a number of obligations on you in the agreement. Read it carefully to be sure of where you stand, and perhaps get your broker to talk you through it. These obligations will include keeping copies of your employees' current driving licences in a safe place and notifying the insurer of any points on their licences or other convictions.

Credit

This covers you against the situation where a customer goes bankrupt while owing you money.

Travel

You'll be used to this from booking your holidays, and this is just the same but it covers you and your staff when you are travelling on business.

Loss of cash

Often important for retailers, this insures against the loss of money from either your premises or while you are transporting it (taking it to the bank, for example).

YOUR BANK

We'll look at the financial products that are available from your bank in the 'Funding your business' section later in this chapter, but here we'll look at the relationship with your bank – important to your financial stability – and your options for switching banks.

The relationship

Let's get one thing straight first of all: you are the customer. Okay, now you understand that, the challenge is getting the bank to understand it! This often comes down to the individual you deal with. Always try to establish a relationship with one person, so that you can build this trust and a normal supplier–customer relationship.

The next thing to get straight is that your bank manager is a sales person for your supplier. They are not your friend or your closest adviser. They want to sell you things, and those things may not always be what you need but what they need to meet their bonus targets. Read the small print closely and ask your accountant for advice before signing anything.

Having said this, a lot of the responsibility for developing a positive relationship with your bank rests on your shoulders. The key things to do are:

● Establish a good relationship with one person at your local branch and always communicate with them. If you are opening a new account, insist on having the meeting with the person who will manage your account day to day.

● If your company is in its early stages, or in a critical phase of growth, provide them with a monthly update, including management accounts and a short written commentary from you about what you are up to. They are unlikely to do much more than skim read this, but what matters is that they can see you are professional and that you are communicating with them. Otherwise provide them with a quarterly or six-monthly update.

- Get in touch with them *as soon* as you know that you may have a cash flow problem that you will need their help to get through. Do not spring last-minute surprises on them – or, even worse, keep quiet and hope they won't notice you going overdrawn.

- Be polite and try not to laugh in their face when they attempt to sell you an insurance policy that is twice the price of the more comprehensive policy arranged by your broker. (I'm only half joking by putting this on the list.)

Switching banks

There are a range of different business bank accounts available, so you don't need to restrict yourself to the usual suspects – HSBC, Barclays, Lloyds TSB and Natwest. Lots of the smaller banks and building societies are seeking to compete in this market and are offering good deals.

You can see, and compare, different accounts at **www.moneyfactsonline.co.uk/mfbaf.**

Once you've checked the deals on offer, you can try to negotiate with your current bank for a better deal, or you can switch banks. This is a much more straightforward process since a Competition Commission report strongly criticized the banks. The transfer will be smooth and fast, and even your direct debits will be transferred automatically (in theory).

Complaining

If you want to raise a complaint about your bank you must first complain to them. If your complaint is not resolved to your satisfaction using their complaints procedure, you can take it to the Financial Ombudsman if your turnover is less than £1m. Your bank must provide you with contact details for the Ombudsman, but you can also find information at **www.financial-ombudsman.org.uk.**

PLANNING

As an entrepreneur you'll find that careful planning can put you well ahead of your competitors and give you a much greater chance of business survival. In terms of finance, however, planning is absolutely critical.

Business plan

Every business should have some form of basic plan for the year ahead. If you're planning to raise money you'll need to have a full blown business plan. Even if you're not seeking to convince any outsiders of the merits of your business I recommend having a mini business plan, which actually tells the story of what you plan to do and how you plan to do it, alongside the figures themselves. You and your management team need this to guide you in running the business, as numbers are only half the story of a company.

Richard Stutely's book *The Definitive Business Plan* (Financial Times Prentice Hall) is an excellent guide, especially if you're running anything quite complex. I suggest you work through his book – it's what I used to write the business plan for my companies.

The financial elements of your business plan will include a Profit Forecast for at least a year. If you are presenting the plan to raise funding, however, you will be expected to show at least two or three years of profit forecast – though any years after the second don't need to be broken down to show month by month totals, just the summary for the year.

Tool

Profit Forecast

Your business plan should include a Profit Forecast (accountants usually call this a Profit and Loss Forecast, but hey, we're positive-thinking entrepreneurs!).

Most start-up businesses incur losses in their start-up phase, which can last months or years depending on the type of business. The most important thing is to achieve a manageable cash flow.

A Profit Forecast shows the income and expenditure in the business as it is incurred – recorded at the point at which the invoice is received or sent for costs or sales respectively.

The forecast includes the following sections down the left hand side of the page.

Sales

It's best to break this section down a bit with a line for each product type – but you don't need to go as far as a line for every single product! For example, if you were an IT business you'd have a line each for 'Hardware Sales', 'Software Sales', 'Support Contracts', 'Installation Fees'. Under all these put a line for 'Total Sales'.

You may want to start by using a separate sheet to do some calculations in order to get a more accurate forecast. List all your services and products, and the number of units or hours you plan to sell for each item in each month. Then multiply these by the unit prices. This will give you a better idea of what the totals should be.

Cost of Sales

These are any costs that you incur in order to fulfil a sale. They include the cost of any products that you would buy in. So, in the example of our IT company, if they planned to sell a network of 20 computers, they would have Cost of Sales that include buying in 20 computers, a server, software and network cables from their suppliers at trade prices. Again, summarize these by type of product or service rather than listing every possible item, and then put a total underneath this section.

Contribution

This is often referred to by accountants as 'Gross Profit', but I don't like to start bandying the 'P' word around just yet – because there are plenty of costs still to come! What this section shows is what contribution your sales are making to the overheads and profits of the business. In other words, the income that is left once the Cost of Sales has been accounted for.

So, to find this figure out for each month on your plan, subtract the Total Cost of Sales from the Total Sales.

Overheads

In this section you list all the costs of the business that have to be paid whether or not you make any sales. This section will include lines for Rent, Salaries, Employer's tax/NI, Expenses, Telephone, Light/Heat/Power, Stationery/Postage, etc.

You may also need to include depreciation on any capital expenditure. (This is the purchase of machinery, IT or other high value items that you will use over a number of years. Depreciation means that if a computer cost £900 and will last you three years, you might only show the cost of £300 in each of those three years on your Profit Forecast instead of taking the full cost of £900 in year 1.) It should be noted that HM Revenue and Customs have rules on the rates of depreciation allowed for calculating taxable profits. You do not have to use the same rates in your management accounts but it makes things simpler. Now, total up all your overheads at the bottom.

Profit Before Interest and Tax (PBIT)

This single line simply shows the result of subtracting your overheads from your contribution. Hopefully it's positive!

►

Interest

Here you show the interest that you will be charged on any bank loans, overdrafts, etc., and any interest that you will receive from investments.

Profit Before Tax

This is generally the final line on the Profit Forecast – and you've probably guessed that it simply shows your PBIT minus the Total Interest.

A Profit Forecast is included as part of the Financial Forecast template on the CD-Rom.

Profit is, of course, important in planning your business success, but it becomes irrelevant if you run out of cash. Cash is the fuel for your business – if you run out of it you come crashing back to Earth. To avoid this you need to plan your cash flow carefully.

Tool

Cash Flow Forecast

Your Cash Flow Forecast is divided into the following three sections: Income, Expenditure and Financing.

Under the 'Income' heading you put all your sales income, but also income from any equipment or other assets you plan to sell, at the time you expect to receive the cash.

Under the 'Expenditure' heading you put all the costs that you have to pay out, including to suppliers for the goods you bought under the Cost of Sales in the Profit Forecast, as well as the costs in the Overheads section except non-cash items such as depreciation. You should add in the full costs of any capital expenditure you expect to make. Put these in at the point at which you expect to have to pay the cash out.

Under the 'Financing' heading you list any cash that your business receives or pays out in relation to the funding of the company. So this might include investment into the company by shareholders, receiving a bank loan, repayments on a bank loan, etc. Also include a separate line showing payments of interest on financing. Show any payments out as negative amounts.

Following these three sections you have a three-line summary:

- Opening Balance. This is the amount of cash that you have at the start of the month.

- Cash Flow. This is the total of Income, minus Expenditure, plus Financing. It will be a positive number if cash flows into your business during the month, or a negative number if cash flows out of the company in the period.

- Closing Balance. This is the Opening Balance plus the Cash Flow. This amount is then carried forward to be the next month's
  Opening Balance.

If there are months where the Closing Balance is negative, this indicates that you need to find extra financing for your business by making more sales in that period, collecting money earlier, increasing prices, paying suppliers later by arrangement, or arranging an overdraft with your bank. Alternatively, you can seek to reduce or delay expenditure.

The main difference between your Cash Flow Forecast and your Profit Forecast is that figures are not recorded at the point of invoice, but at the point of payment. That means you forecast sales income into the plan at the point at which the money will actually clear into your bank account and be available to spend, and you forecast expenditure at the point at which you will have to pay for items.

There are a few other key differences:

1. Generally, if you are registered for VAT, your Profit Forecast won't include VAT because you simply collect it from your customers and pay it to HMRC minus the VAT you are reclaiming, so it doesn't affect your profits. It does affect your Cash Flow, however, so you include VAT on any sales amounts and any purchases, and you have a line in your forecast showing the VAT that you are due to pay to (or reclaim from) HMRC.

2. Do not include depreciation in your Cash Flow Forecast, but do include the actual cost of any capital expenditure you plan to make.

A Cash Flow Forecast is included as part of the Financial Forecast template on the CD-Rom.

A bank or investor may also require a balance sheet as part of your plans. This shows the assets and liabilities of the business at a fixed point in time. In a forecast this might show the balance sheet at the end of each month in the plan. Your bookkeeper or accountant can help with preparation of a balance sheet.

The first year of your plan will be your budget for the coming year.

Management cash flow

Having a Cash Flow Forecast for the year is all very well to give yourself and your investors a picture of what the business is *likely* to do, but rest assured it will bear absolutely no relation to what does *actually* happen in the end.

The challenge is that you can make a plan in November that looks great, but in March your biggest competitor announces a price cut, or your main supplier raises their prices. You can't foresee everything in your plans.

Plans are still worth making, because otherwise you are wandering without direction, but you need to revisit your plans constantly to adjust the assumptions, to take account of progress to date and to take account of the effects of outside influences.

The key part of your plan that needs to be reworked on a regular basis is your Cash Flow Forecast. In more established businesses that are doing well this can be done on a monthly basis, but in smaller businesses, or those who are going through tough times, a weekly Cash Flow Forecast is needed.

This should extend for at least three months, and every time a week passes you should add a new week's forecast at the end of the plan. This is called a 'rolling' forecast.

You'll find a template for a Management Cash Flow on the CD-Rom.

REPORTING

Annual accounts

If you are self-employed or run your business as a partnership, it can be a great help to have your financial year run to 31 March and make your accounts up to this date. This then ties in better with the tax year and can save you a lot of time on paperwork.

If you run your business as a limited company, then it matters less when your financial year runs to. Some people like the clarity of having it the same as a calendar year, others like to tie it in to the tax year by running it to 31 March.

When you register a new company at Companies House, you will be allocated a year-end date 12 months later. You can change this to be the date you wish by obtaining form 225, completing it and returning it to Companies House.

Once your year-end passes you need to begin the process of preparing your annual accounts. This is a legal requirement for limited companies, and they must be filed at Companies House within ten months of your year-end.

If you have a turnover of less than £1m and assets of less than £1.4m then you do not need to have these accounts audited (checked in detail by a specially registered accountant).

Also, if you qualify as a 'Small Company' you only need to file the following with Companies House:

- An abbreviated balance sheet.
- Accompanying notes.
- Special auditors' report (if applicable – see audit exemption above).

To qualify as a Small Company you must meet at least two of these criteria for the current and previous financial year:

- Annual turnover of less than £5.6m.
- Assets of less than £2.8m.
- Less than 50 employees (averaged over the year).

However, it's still worth producing a full set of accounts for your own use (and your bank and investors may want to see them).

If you qualify as a 'Medium Company' you only need to file the following documents with Companies House:

- Full Balance Sheet.
- Abbreviated Profit and Loss Account.
- Directors' report, note to the accounts.
- Special auditors' report.

To qualify as a Medium Company you must meet at least two of these criteria in the current and previous financial year:

- Annual turnover of less than £22.8m.
- Assets of less than £11.4m.
- Less than 250 employees (averaged over the year).

If you don't qualify as a Small or Medium Company, your accountant will need to prepare 'full' accounts and you will need to file these at Companies House.

In order to prepare these accounts, your accountant will need all your key paperwork from the last 12 months, including:

- Your bank statements for all bank accounts.

- All sales invoices.

- All purchase invoices (sent to you by your suppliers).

- A list of all cheques you issued during the year and what they were for.

- A list of work in progress at the year-end.

- A list of shareholders and how many shares they own, as well as any they acquired or sold during the year.

- Your VAT returns.

- Details of your PAYE payments.

Insider Knowledge

Your accountant charges by the hour, so you can save yourself a lot of money by giving them the information in a clear, well-presented way. Your accountant may be telling you not to worry about it, he'll have someone sort out your shoebox of receipts – but that person will just be a trainee or a secretary doing all the boring monotonous jobs, and you will be billed anything upwards of £35 an hour for the privilege. You'd be better off hiring a temp yourself to sort it out and paying the agency £10 an hour. But, even better, keep your records in good order in the first place!

Management accounts

For small businesses a Profit Statement (again, accountants normally call this a Profit and Loss Statement) and a Cash Flow Statement are enough for the management of the company to be able to monitor progress against the plan each month.

The Profit Statement takes the same format as the Profit Forecast, but for just the one month, and shows what the actual figures were compared to those in your budget.

One option for the Cash Flow Statement is for it simply to list the differences between the Profit Statement and the movement of cash in the business. So it would have a line to remove depreciation, a line to add in capital expenditure, a line to subtract any invoices that were raised in the period but not paid in the period, a line to add in any invoices that were not raised in the period but were paid in the period, and so on. It's just a line by line reconciliation of the Profit Statement with the actual movement of money in the month.

The other option for the Cash Flow Statement is to present it just like one month of your Cash Flow Forecast, and this makes it easier to compare actual results against your budget.

You then present the figures, along with an updated forecast for the next three months, at your management and/or board meetings and discuss any major differences between budget and actual in the results. What can you learn? Any warning signs? Are there any changes that you should make in the business? What about the forecasts? Any problems ahead?

In a larger business you will need to prepare more detailed management accounts that show the Profit Statement and the Cash Flow Statement for the period, along with the revised forecast for the next three months and a Balance Sheet.

Key performance indicators

It's not enough just to study what has happened with the money in your business, you also need to look at important trends in the business, and whether you are meeting certain milestones.

You can do this by using key performance indicators. You simply choose what three to five things are important for you to monitor and ask your bookkeeper or finance manager to gather the information monthly to report to the management and/or the board.

These could include:

● Number of new customers.

● Average order value.

● Days that customers take to pay after invoice.

A range of other factors may also be important in your industry, or for the stage of development of your company.

FUNDING YOUR BUSINESS

Funding your business isn't something that only needs doing at start-up – you constantly need to look ahead at your cash flow for any potential funding requirement and put it in place in plenty of time. You also need to fund growth in terms of new machinery, new staff, extra marketing and so on.

In my book *How to Fund your Business*, published by Prentice Hall Business, I go into much more detail about your options for sourcing funding, how to choose between them and how to secure the money, but here is a summary of some of the key methods for funding your business.

Sales

This is the best way of funding your business but one that is strangely often overlooked. If you can see that you're going to need to raise some extra cash in your business in a month or two, then organize some special offers to move extra stock. Approach a few key customers to offer them a special deal for ordering early, ordering more or paying early.

Overdrafts

This is an expensive way to borrow money and is only suitable for short term requirements. It is often worth having a facility agreed with your bank, even if you don't plan to use it. Then you are prepared if a customer pays late or some other short term event happens that affects your cash flow. Do not be tempted to use this facility constantly though. It will cost you a fortune and earn you a bad 'behaviour' score on your bank's computer (an internal measure only, which is not shared with the credit agencies), which can make it difficult to get what you want from the bank in other areas. Overdrafts are designed for occasional use, and the bank likes to see you regularly going into credit.

Insider Knowledge

One piece of small print that often catches out entrepreneurs when it comes to overdrafts is that they are repayable 'in full on demand'. This means that the bank manager can write to you tomorrow to say they are removing your overdraft facility and that you must immediately pay in to bring your account into credit. They will not hesitate to do this if they get worried about the state of your company finances.

Loans

This form of funding is often used to help a business expand. Banks often like to match a loan to investment from the founders or other investors, so you may be required to put some money in at the same time, take a drop in salary or make some other 'investment in kind'. Bank managers often have very short and selective memories, and may not take into account the thousands of pounds you may have put in just last year.

Remember that a loan comes with repayments – and with payments of interest. You need to be sure that you can afford these payments. Plan your cash flow very carefully, and look at what will happen if your sales come in 10 per cent, 20 per cent or even 40 per cent lower than forecast.

The banks can come down on you very hard if things don't go to plan and you are unable to make some repayments on time.

When you apply for a loan the bank will want to see a detailed business plan, including cash flow forecasts. They are also likely to want some security, such as a personal guarantee or a charge over machinery or stock. Avoid personal guarantees, or giving your own home as security. Do not mix your personal finances into the business to this extent. If you really feel you must then be certain to get professional advice – do not take this step lightly.

Insider Knowledge

The banks like you to feel that there is no room for negotiation in any deal they offer you, but there always is. Negotiate everything. They can improve the interest rate, waive certain charges and remove certain demands for security. Bank managers have often insisted on personal guarantees in granting loans or overdrafts to businesses I have been involved in, but I have always refused point blank. I never ever give personal guarantees. At the end of the day, they will give in if they want the sale. Remember you are the customer and they make money if you buy their products – they are not doing you a favour!

The government, through the Department for Trade and Industry, operates The Small Firms Loan Guarantee Scheme. Under the scheme the government will provide a guarantee (security) to the bank to secure a loan for your business. There are criteria that you must meet. Most high street banks can provide loans under this scheme. You can find out more about the scheme at **www.dti.gov.uk/sflg**.

Asset finance

This is a common way of funding any capital expenditure you need in your business such as vehicles, IT equipment or machinery. There are a range of options available to you, including hire purchase or leasing. Your bank will offer asset finance packages, but you will get a better deal from specialist asset finance companies – and often the company you are purchasing from will have some deals already in place with finance companies. Get professional advice from your accountant.

Leasing is a bit like renting a piece of equipment, while hire purchase means that you are making staged payments to the finance company, and once these are completed you own the asset. Even though you'll have paid much more for it in the end than if you had bought it outright at the start, you'll have had the advantages of a better cash flow.

Debt factoring

This can be a good way for some companies to improve their cash flow. It involves 'selling' your invoices to a finance company for up to 85 per cent of their face value. They then collect the payment on these invoices, at which time they pay you the remainder of the money minus their fees and interest.

Interest charged is generally better than bank overdraft rates. Charges are about 0.75 per cent to 2.5 per cent of the amount factored, depending on your turnover, the status of your customers and other criteria.

The main banks offer debt factoring services, but they are generally more expensive than other specialist providers.

Again, get your accountant's advice if you are considering factoring.

Equity

Raising finance by selling shares in your business is a form of finance that is restricted to limited companies (as partnerships and sole traders don't have shares to sell).

You may choose to sell shares to:

- Friends and family.
- Management and staff (be careful about tax implications).
- Business angels.
- Venture capitalists.

Insider Knowledge

You can make your company more attractive for friends and family, as well as business angels, by registering under the Enterprise Investment Scheme (EIS). This allows the investor to claim back a proportion of their investment against their tax bill – effectively giving them a profit in year 1. Then, if the worst happens and your business fails, they can reclaim a further amount against their tax bill. Essentially it only means they are risking half their money. EIS is a fantastic scheme and has helped many entrepreneurial companies to raise funding from business angels (including some of mine). The scheme is very, very easy to set up and administer. Ask your accountant for details.

I recommend equity as one of the best ways for entrepreneurial companies to raise money, and this is particularly true if you have ambitious plans. Some entrepreneurs are funny about letting other people have shares in their company, fearing that they are giving up 'control'. My view is that you release even more control in your business by being in debt to traditional lenders.

Equity investors can also bring expertise and contacts to your business, leading to this form of funding being termed 'Intelligent Money'.

RECORD-KEEPING

Good record-keeping can not only prevent you from being fined by the authorities, it can also help you grow your business smoothly, with the correct information always at hand to make decisions.

What the law requires

You must keep accurate financial records in your business for at least six years.

These include:

- Cheque book stubs.

- Paying-in books.

- Bank statements.

- Sales invoices.

- Purchase invoices.

- Receipts for expenses or cash purchases.

- Copies of VAT returns.

- Details of all salary payments made.

- Details of all PAYE and National Insurance Contributions paid to HMRC.

These records must be kept safe and must be available for inspection by HMRC

What can help you

Using an accountant or bookkeeper

Entrepreneurs are most useful to the business when they are selling to customers or providing a service to the customer and motivating the rest of the team to do the same. Any time that they spend doing accounts or filling in forms is lost time. For that reason I highly recommend that you consider getting a freelance bookkeeper to come and do your books once a week, fortnight or month, depending on the amount of work required.

This will not only free up your time, it will also ensure that your business has more accurate records and is better prepared for growth. Fast growing companies are often tripped up by not being able to keep a track of everything – especially cash – as they grow. Having an experienced bookkeeper will help you avoid many of the potential pitfalls.

You should also appoint an accountant to do your annual accounts and to deal with HMRC on Corporation Tax.

You can decide whether it's best to have your accountant or bookkeeper handle payroll and PAYE, VAT and so on. You can also choose to use a specialist payroll bureau to handle this task.

Using accounting software

There are a few different accountancy software packages available, and your accountant/bookkeeper will have a preferred system. This is likely to be Sage (particularly for accountants, as they earn money from Sage for selling the software to you!), but other systems are available, including Quickbooks and Mamut. Shop around and see which system best suits your needs.

CHAPTER FOUR
Running your business

We've looked at the fundamental parts of every business:

- Sales and customers.

- Employing people.

- Managing the money.

These three things are what will take up most of your time and energy. However, there are a range of other things that need to be done in any small business not just to administer the business, and keep it going, but also to help it grow and prosper. That's what we'll look at in this chapter.

PROCEDURES AND TEMPLATES

This is one of the secrets that small business can take from big business and put into action in a much more effective and productive way.

Big companies have standard contracts, standard letters and standard forms. Unfortunately, they haven't refined these to be as simple as possible – they have designed them to cover all possible eventualities. Big companies put standard documents in place to make sure that the idiots they believe they employ on the front line don't screw up – and to create a paper-trail in order to work out who's fault it was when they do screw up. That means they're complex instead of straightforward, and people hate using them.

A small company can develop these standard documents, but you're doing it to make life easier, and repetitive tasks quicker, for the clever people you employ on the front line, because it's far better to maximize their time doing other things. Developing the forms for this reason means you'll make them as simple and user friendly as possible.

Having standard documents also means that it's easier for new members of the team to quickly get up to speed and do work to the same standard as anyone else. In addition, customers will get a more standard level of service, regardless of which team member deals with them.

Here are some things you can do:

1. Standard contracts for the key types of work you do for customers.

2. Standard contracts for staff.

3. Template letters for each stage of the sales process – but make sure that sales people can customize them in individual cases if they wish.

4. Standard forms for capturing details about potential new customers.

5. Standard sales order forms.

You and your team should also keep the idea of standardization in mind and look for other letters that you regularly send out. Could they be turned into a template for other people to use?

Checklists are a good way to standardize procedures. For each instance of a particular event, the team member takes a checklist sheet, puts a reference at the top (customer name, account number, etc.) and then works through the checklist, ticking things off as they are done. You could use this for:

1. Managing the sales process from first enquiry to first order.

2. Managing the targeting of new sales prospects.

3. Managing the provision of a product or service.

Once you've developed these standard forms, contracts, letters and checklists, train people in how to use them. Be ready to change them based on feedback from the people who use them.

GATHERING INTELLIGENCE

As well as the work you have already done, you'll constantly need to be gathering intelligence on external factors that affect your business to feed into your planning process. This doesn't mean tapping the phones of your competitors or using private investigators – it means just using basic information gathering methods to ensure that you know about any potential opportunities or problems.

Information you want

You want to monitor news about your customers, suppliers, competitors and your market in general. As well as looking for any positive developments, you need to be on the look out for any potential problems.

On top of problems from suppliers or competitors, external problems for your business can come from the following areas:

1. Political. New laws or regulations might be introduced. These could specifically affect your industry, or relate more generally to your business, such as Health and Safety or Data Protection regulations. The government's shifting policy may also affect what grants or subsidies are available, or the ability of foreign competitors to enter your market.

2. Economic. Interest rate changes will affect the cost of borrowing or investments that your company may have. Taxes will affect your profitability and competitiveness. What would happen to your business if there's a slowdown in the housing market, a general slowdown in the economy, or even a recession? What would happen if there was an economic boom? How do currency exchange rates affect your business?

3. Social. Fashions and trends come and go. What's the next big thing? How are public tastes and attitudes changing? What about the social pressures on your target market? Are they working fewer hours, taking more holidays, starting families later, etc.? What does this mean for your business?

4. Technological. Depending on your industry, this may be the area you need to watch most closely as things can change so quickly. What will the new technology be for your industry? What will your competitors be using? What new technology will be available to your customers, and how will that affect what they want from you? Can you deliver elements of your services over the internet or mobile networks? How can technology help you to become more efficient and competitive?

5. Environmental. This can be environmental in a broad sense: What will global warming, changing weather, warmer winters or rainier summers mean for your business? It could also relate to your local environment: what new buildings are planned and how will that affect your business? What other changes might be about to happen in your area?

6. Competitive. This is the key one. Your competitors will be actively working against you, trying to launch products that are better than yours, trying to target your customers and so on. What are they up to now? What are they planning? What are they just thinking about? What trade shows will they be exhibiting at? What advertising campaigns are they running? What press coverage are they getting? Are they recruiting or laying off staff? How are customers reacting to their work? You get the picture – anything you can find out about your competitors helps to build a picture about what they are doing.

These six headings are known as the PESTEC framework, which is well known amongst bank managers, accountants and consultants. (Many of them might use the 'C' to denote 'Cultural', but I believe this to be covered by 'Social' and that Competitive is an important area of threats to examine. I'm just explaining that so you can respond to any questions about it from your business advisers!)

Where to find it

There are many sources of information that can be useful to your business and that you should consider as sources of intelligence on opportunities – and on the threats outlined in the PESTEC framework. Here are some ideas to get you started.

Google

This internet search engine has become a fantastic way to research the information you need. It allows you to search websites as well as a wide range of online news sources with the Google News service. But what's even better is that you can set up Google Alerts. These will send you daily or weekly updates by email on search terms that you have set up, so you can put your company name, and your competitors' company and product names in, as search terms and then receive updates every time a new web page or news story is found. To set up Google Alerts (for free), go to **www.google.co.uk/alerts**.

Newspapers

I highly recommend getting the **Financial Times** newspaper. Because of its business focus you get analysis of the main news stories that impact on companies, but it also reports on what a lot of the large companies are doing in terms of market strategy, acquisitions and so on. If you buy from, sell to or compete with public companies, it can be an invaluable source of information about them.

General business and trade magazines

Subscribe to business magazines and to your industry newsletters and magazines, websites and email newsletters. Then, when they come through, take the step that none of your competitors will be taking and actually read the damn things! Have you seen piles of magazines in people's offices that they plan to read 'one day' but never do? Take yours from that pile on your next train journey, to the dentist's waiting room or anywhere you have some spare time, and that'll put you one step ahead.

Companies House

You can gain access to statutory documents filed by your customers, suppliers and competitors via the Companies House website at **www.companieshouse.co.uk** and selecting the Webcheck service. This allows you to view their accounts and any other important documents relating to share transactions, director appointments and resignations, and so on.

Get out there!

Go to trade shows, conferences and other events in your industry. It's amazing what you can learn at them. Chat to your customers about the industry and their other suppliers. Chat to your suppliers about their other customers. Be chatty with people and they'll be chatty with you – giving you all the unpublished industry gossip.

Information markets

This is like betting on particular outcomes and is therefore a fun way of getting your team or your customers involved in your planning and research. You could run a bet in which people predict how many units of a certain product you will sell this year, and how many your key competitors will sell. It's amazing what knowledge or gut instinct groups of people share that don't come out in their normal work.

These information markets are amazingly accurate. The CIA was even planning to launch one to predict terrorist attacks, until a political controversy about gambling erupted!

There are regulations governing the running of betting operations, so you'd need to make it for fun prizes (everyone with the correct answer, or the nearest answer, will be entered into a draw for a day off, or the use of the boss's car for a day, etc.).

Red Team planning

This is something that military planners use to predict enemy actions. It's all too easy to pretend that your opposition are stupid people who will just wait to react to what you do rather than coming up with their own clever plans. The best way to avoid this is to split your team in half for planning sessions (you can split into more teams if you have multiple competitors and enough team members). One team (the 'Blue' Team) plan as if they are your company, while the other team (the 'Red' Team) plan the actions of a particular competitor. They should receive a full briefing on your competitor's products, services, customers and so on, and then use all their intelligence, all their background knowledge and all their deviousness to try to beat your Blue Team. You will get the best results from this if you have your very best talent on the Red Team. This can be a great exercise for a team building away day. Once the exercise is over, bring the groups together as one again and examine what you've learnt about your competitor and what they could do to provide the biggest challenge to you. How can you all plan together to reduce that threat?

But don't get too stuck into just being ready to react to what they might do – use the knowledge to build on your proactive plans. Attack rather than defend!

When you gather all this intelligence, you'll need somewhere to keep it. Perhaps start a file for each competitor, or add customer information to their customer file. You might want to keep the information online or on your network in a Knowledgebase that's searchable by your team (ask your IT whizzkids).

COMPANY MEETINGS

In order to run your company there are three levels of meetings that need to be held. There are, of course, many other meetings that will be held in order to carry out the work of the company, but these three types of meeting focus on the way the company is run as an organization. They are management meetings, board meetings and the Annual General Meeting.

Management Meetings

As your company grows, you should have a key team of managers who help you run the company, with each one taking responsibility for a particular area of the business.

It can help the business greatly for this team to meet on a weekly basis. However, it doesn't have to be in person each week – it could be on a telephone conference. I would suggest meeting in person once a month as a minimum though.

These meetings should be brief and well chaired – and that's your job! Set an agenda for the meeting and stick to it.

Tool

Agenda

Whenever you are preparing an agenda for a meeting at any level, you need to do it in a planned and considered way, because this document has a huge impact on the effectiveness of the meeting. Without a good agenda the discussion will wander off all over the place, nothing will get decided and the meeting will run late.

For each item on the agenda, state whether it is:

- **Presentation.** A person at the meeting will present information. No discussion! Put down who will be presenting this information to the meeting. For example, 'Alice to outline market research for USA'.

- **Report.** A document has been submitted in advance for people to read before the meeting and will simply be accepted onto the record of the meeting at this point. For example, 'Report into Japanese market'.

- **Questions.** People at the meeting may ask specific questions to the person who has given a presentation, or the author of a report, that was a previous agenda item. Specify what questions may be about. For example, 'Questions about the Japanese market report'.

- **Debate.** An issue will be debated at the meeting. Specify what the question to be debated is. For example, 'Should we target the USA, Japan or Australia as our first export market?'

- **Decision.** This is an item in which you, the chairman, will ask for a vote on a particular decision. Put down the matter to be decided and the possible options. For example, 'Which export market to target first: USA, Japan or Australia'.

You should also set a time limit for each item. As the chairman it'll be your responsibility to keep the meeting to this time limit, and that'll help ensure you finish on time – another important discipline!

A sample agenda document is included on the CD-Rom in the back of this book.

In essence, the management meetings should focus on the day to day issues of running the business: people issues, such as recruitment, retention, motivation, discipline, etc.; sales issues; customer issues; and resources issues.

Board meetings

In a very small company, this meeting might be a lonely affair, with just you and the cat, but it is still worth having. Take this time to go through what is happening in the business and you will soon find it invaluable.

As you grow, however, it is well worth bringing other people onto the board, particularly non-executive directors (people who don't work in the business). We'll look at this subject shortly.

In my view, it's ideal to have between three and five people on the board in an entrepreneurial company, as having too many can slow things down into a committee-like process. But don't just seek people who will agree with you! The most valuable contribution the board can make is to help you see things differently and to challenge your thinking.

Some companies have monthly board meetings, while others find that quarterly meetings are better. It all depends on how quickly your business is growing or whether there are any ongoing problems.

Whichever you decide is best for your company, you need to plan your board meeting properly to get any benefit from it. It's all too easy for individual directors to get side-tracked onto minor issues that are particular favourites for them, but which are not the most important to discuss.

Once again, the agenda is an important tool here. Remember that your board meeting is not intended to be about the day to day running of the company – it's about long term strategy.

The board meeting is the place to compare the monthly management accounts with the budget and look at trends of beating or missing the budget. Your board can also assess how well the business is delivering on the expectations of founders, investors, talent and customers.

A sample Board Agenda is included on the CD-Rom.

You must also keep minutes of board meetings. These are simply a record of who was present and what the decisions were.

As I mentioned, the board is doing its job best if it is asking you difficult questions and challenging your thinking. Don't feel intimidated or defensive; give consideration to their points and either explain why you don't agree or allow yourself to be persuaded.

Building on my favourite analogy linking business with aeroplanes, the board is air traffic control. They don't tell you which buttons to press when, but they help make sure you don't crash and that you are headed in the right direction for where you want to go.

Non-executive directors

These are people from outside the business that you recruit to provide a different view at your board meetings. They may also bring contacts, industry knowledge and sometimes even new investment into your company.

Their main contribution is making sure that the business has a proper direction and is being properly managed. They will challenge you, they will question your decisions, but it is all for the good of the business.

You can find non-executive directors for your business in the following ways:

- Asking a local business person you respect to be one.

- Asking someone who is experienced in your industry and you respect to be one.

- Using a service such as **www.directorbank.com**.

You will normally have to pay non-executive directors, and fees vary greatly depending on their experience and current commitments. But some people are interested in being able to make investments in entre-preneurial companies with a lot of potential and will then seek to become a non-executive director to watch over their investment. They often won't charge a fee for this as they are more interested in growing their investment.

Responsibilities of directors

A company director is responsible for the proper running of the com-pany for the benefit of all shareholders. The position comes with a number of legal and other obligations and some stiff penalties if you don't carry them out. All limited companies must have at least one director.

The legal obligations are to:

- Ensure the company files annual accounts at Companies House and provides a report to shareholders at least 21 days before the Annual General Meeting.

- Ensure the company files the Annual Return and other required documents that may be necessary at Companies House.

- Ensure the company complies with all relevant laws, such as those on Health and Safety, Employment, the Data Protection Act and other legislation.

- Ensure the company meets its obligations with regard to reporting its tax liability, performing other duties under tax legislation and paying tax.

You are also expected to meet certain standards as a company director. You must carry out your role with a level of skill that can reasonably be expected of someone with your experience and training, and as if it were your own personal business (which it probably is in your case!). You must remember that you are acting on behalf of all the shareholders and must not favour any one (for example, if you own 80 per cent of the company and an investor owns 20 per cent, you must make decisions based on the best interests of both of you).

There are very onerous penalties that can be imposed on directors who fail in their duties or who are found to have acted improperly. You can be personally fined, and could even be sent to prison for some offences. Of course, this is extremely rare and you would have to have done something very serious. But as with all parts of life, it's in your control to make sure you stay on the right side of the law. Make sure you study your obligations and meet them.

Responsibilities of the company secretary

Company law is being reviewed as I write this, and it looks likely that the requirement for all companies to have a company secretary will be removed in the near future. Look on the updates section of the FlyingStartups website to find out the latest, at **www.flyingstartups.com/updates**.

In a small business there isn't much need for a company secretary, as there simply isn't much formal administration to do. Don't let the word 'secretary' confuse you though – they don't do the typing or open the post. Company secretaries carry out a lot of the legal obligations of the company in terms of maintaining key documents and filing them with Companies House. This is the legal responsibility of the directors, but the directors delegate this to the official company secretary.

A company secretary can also be a director of the company, but not the sole director. So if you are running a one person company then it's quite common to ask your husband or wife to be company secretary as a formality, but you or your accountant actually does the work.

You can also hire a specialist company to be your company secretary, and this can be a particularly wise move if you are a fast growing company or have at least grown past the early stages. They will oversee all of the legal obligations of the business with their professional eye, taking away many of the potential pitfalls. You can find a chartered secretary at **www.icsa.org.uk**.

The administration that a company secretary will normally be responsible for is as follows:

- To give formal notice of board meetings and shareholder meetings (normally the Annual General Meeting).

- To arrange for minutes to be taken at these meetings.

- To keep important legal documents safe, such as the Certificate of Incorporation and the Memorandum and Articles of Association.

- To keep the company's register of all people to have held the position of director or company secretary.

- To keep the company's register of all shareholdings that have been, or continue to be, held in the company, including the details of the shareholder.

- To keep a register with details of any shares or other financial interests in the company that are held by directors.

- To keep an official register of anyone who holds a debenture over the company's assets, such as a bank or other finance provider.

- To file the company's Annual Return at Companies House.

- To ensure that the company files its annual accounts within ten months of its financial year-end.

- To file necessary documents at Companies House whenever a new director or secretary is appointed, resigns or changes their contact details.

- To notify Companies House of any change in the registered address of the company.

- To issue shareholders with share certificates when they invest in the company.

These are the main obligations, but there are other forms that need to be filed in certain circumstances. Your accountant can give you further advice.

Annual General Meetings

Again, this is an area of company law that is currently under review, but at present all limited companies have to hold an Annual General Meeting (AGM) open to all shareholders.

The main requirements for AGMs are as follows:

- If you are in the very early stages of your company then you must hold your first AGM within 18 months of incorporation. After that, they ought to be held annually, but must be no later than 15 months after the previous AGM.

- You must notify all shareholders and all directors of the meeting by writing to them at least 21 days in advance. You must provide them with copies of the annual accounts by this deadline too.

- Formal minutes of the meeting must be taken. Once approved, they must be signed by the Chairman.

When the AGM is held, there are certain formalities that must be observed:

- A vote must be held to approve the accounts.

- A vote must be held to approve the appointment of the auditors (if the company is required to have its accounts audited).

- Votes may be needed to reappoint directors, or to appoint new directors, depending on the regulations in your Memorandum and Articles of Association.

- You may need to hold votes to pass special or extraordinary resolutions. If you do this, then you must file copies of any such resolutions that are passed at Companies House.

These are the basic legal requirements of an AGM. However, you can use it to give a real insight into your company's work and progress to your shareholders, and to excite them about the future ahead. Then, how about a party?

SHAREHOLDERS

Shareholders are the owners of your company. That may just be you, or you and some co-founders – or you may have sold shares to raise money for your business. Shares are a fundamental principle of the limited company and can be a powerful tool to help fast growing companies raise finance and reward staff.

What shares are

They're just a little bit of paper but they can be worth a fortune. Shares show ownership of a limited company. That company can be a public limited company, but we're going to focus on the most common example, the private limited company.

When you registered the limited company you will have drafted, or been given by the registration agent, an official document called a Memorandum of Association. This sets out what the authorized share capital of the company is. This might say:

'The authorized share capital of the company is £1,000. This is divided into 1,000 shares of £1 each.'

This means that, as it presently stands, the company may issue up to 1,000 shares, with a *nominal* value of £1. A nominal value does not restrict what price you can sell the shares at, as the shares should become more valuable as the company grows. You can sell the shares for any value that you and an investor agree between you, but the face value is always £1.

Issuing shares

Whenever new shares are issued, this dilutes the ownership, and therefore the value of the existing shareholders. If the company is growing enough, or if the new investment adds enough value to the company, they may not mind. Consider the following example. The company has so far issued 100 shares and you own them all. You have invited someone to join you in the business and have agreed with them that they will invest £25,000 to buy 50 per cent of the company (the company is very small at this stage!). You then issue them with 100 shares in return for their money, meaning that there are now 200 shares issued. That means you now own 50 per cent of what you owned before – but the company's value has just gone up by £25,000.

Therefore, you have to agree a price for the shares that you feel represents the current value of the business, and that the purchaser feels is a fair valuation for what they are getting, and its future potential growth.

Shares can carry a premium on their value, over and above what anyone sensible would value them at, because of the future potential growth of the business.

So, for example, say you have just set up business in your garden shed and have issued yourself with 100 shares, the company now has a grand total of £100 in its bank account as a result. However, you have discovered how to make gold by refining chicken droppings and you have a panel of prominent scientists who have confirmed your method works. You will now find that people will value your company at significantly more than its balance sheet shows it is worth, which is £100. In this kind of business you could be selling shares with a face value of £1 for millions of pounds each.

Of course, this is an extreme example, but you get the idea.

You don't have to issue all the authorized shares. Alternatively, if you run out of authorized shares as the company grows you can pass a resolution to issue more. Details on what type of resolution will be needed should be set out in your Articles of Association. The increase in authorized share capital will need to be registered at Companies House with a copy of the resolution and a completed form 123.

Offering shares for sale

You might choose to sell shares to family, friends, business angels or even venture capitalists, depending on the stage your company is at. You might even choose to put in a share scheme for your staff as part of your rewards package.

A private limited company is restricted in the ways it can offer shares to people outside the company. It may not make public offerings of shares, and this means that you are restricted in the number of business plans you may send out. You may also only offer shares for sale to experienced or high net worth investors, unless they have some specialist knowledge of your business (i.e. staff, family, friends).

You need to get your accountant's advice on how to comply with these rules in your situation.

Paying dividends

People will want to invest in your business because they think that you are going to:

1. Increase the value of the business by acquiring and creating assets.

2. Generate profits as a result of your business activities.

These can both drive the value of the shares up, but the second point means that there will be surplus money left in the company at the end of the financial year.

Part of this profit can then be distributed to shareholders by means of a dividend. This is a payment of cash back to the owner of each share in the business. So, essentially, the pot of money is divided up according to the percentage of the business each shareholder owns. This money they receive is taxed more lightly than normal income (only Income Tax is charged, not National Insurance Contributions) and so is a tax-efficient way of earning money. For that reason it is the most used way for company founders to take money out of the business.

The company is responsible for paying the tax. The remaining money should then be sent to the shareholder with a statement showing how much tax has been paid on their behalf.

What people can do with your shares

Once people own shares in your business, the shares are their property and they can do whatever they like with them, just as if it was another asset, such as a house.

However, many small companies put in place Shareholder Agreements that limit what shareholders are able to do with their shares. The agreement might give the company or other shareholders first option on buying shares if any shareholder wants to sell, or if the shareholder dies and the shares are passed to their estate.

SUPPLIERS

All businesses depend on their suppliers in order to provide their services or make their products, so finding and managing suppliers is one of the most important activities of your management team.

Finding suppliers

You should regularly review the suppliers who could provide you with a particular service. Look for any new entrants to their market, any changes in the pricing structure and any improvements in technology or quality.

It's well worth considering companies in other countries as suppliers. After years of problems with CD manufacturers in the UK, my company has found a highly reliable supplier in Austria! And although we changed supplier because of quality and service issues, we were very pleasantly surprised to save money too.

There's an online directory of suppliers for a wide variety of products and services at **www.kellysearch.co.uk**.

Another source of potential suppliers is by visiting trade events, networking events and by reading industry newsletters and websites.

Ask potential new suppliers to demonstrate their product or service and provide a quotation. Find out what guarantees they will give on quality and delivery. Do they have minimum order requirements? What are their payment terms? And so on.

But don't select only on price – look for the best value. That is, the best possible service you can get, balanced with the best price. You might decide that it is worth paying more to a new supplier who guarantees to deliver on time.

Handling problems with suppliers

If you find that suppliers are letting you down a little too often, try to sort the problem out amicably at first. Have a chat with your key contact there and get them to look into the problem. It becomes a lot more difficult to achieve anything if you go in with all guns blazing, so be firm but polite and friendly.

If this doesn't achieve the result you want, put your complaint in writing. Avoid the use of emotional language. Stick to the facts and let them speak for themselves. State what it is that you want the supplier to do to put the problem right.

If this still fails you have the remedy of taking your business elsewhere. But the supplier's mistake may have caused you to lose money or may have damaged your business in some other way, and you may have a claim you can make against them. There are some ways of doing this that avoid the huge costs of involving solicitors. You could go to arbitration, where an independent arbitrator will hear the case of each side and then give a decision. You can find out details about this process at **www.arbitrators.org**. If your claim is under £5,000 you could take it to the Small Claims Court (a special track in your local County Court) yourself. The process is designed so that you don't need to involve a solicitor.

DEALING WITH COMMON PROBLEMS

Life doesn't always go smoothly and it's likely that you will have to deal with some common problems as your business grows. Here's some advice on the most common:

1. Our sales are lower than budgeted.

To solve this, start by getting as much feedback from your customers and potential customers as possible. Are your products or services solving their problems or helping them fulfil their dreams? If not, how can you improve them? Often a few small changes can make all the difference. The next thing to examine is whether you have the right channels to market working for you.

Could you use any of the other channels we discussed in Chapter 1, instead of, or in addition to, the channels you are using now? Next, examine how you are establishing the contact with your customers. How do you make them aware that your products or services exist? Could you increase your sales to existing customers by adding services to your products as we discussed in Chapter 1?

Once you're satisfied that you've taken as much action as possible on the steps above, you can begin to examine your pricing. The natural reaction here is to see if you can cut your prices, but before you do this I suggest the opposite. If the quality of your service or your products justifies it, could you increase your prices to aim for the higher end of the market? It may be that you can specialize in a particular area. If you really think a price cut will be the only thing to boost sales then don't actually cut the price, run a series of offers to test this. You need to check that you can increase sales by enough to earn more than you were earning before – so that you're not just increasing the number of units shipped but earning the same money.

Finally, you need to examine the harder facts: do you have the right sales team, do they have the right training, are they generating enough leads, are they following up on leads well enough, and are they closing a high enough percentage of potential sales? Are you targeting the right market? Do you have the right products for the market?

It's best to tackle all these issues as early as possible rather than burying your head in the sand and hoping everything will just sort itself out.

2. **Help, we're running out of cash!**

This is an extremely common problem in small businesses – and it's mainly because our school system shies away from any mention of money in lessons. We just don't get taught about how money works, how to budget, how interest works, how to invest or how to make money work for you. This means that entrepreneurs end up learning all these lessons the hard way – and some learn it in the very hardest way possible, by going bust.

You need to forecast your cash flow constantly and always keep the forecast up to date. That gives you more time to prepare for any potential problems. If you do then spot a problem looming the steps to consider are:

a) Can you make any extra sales to customers before that crunch point?

b) Can you persuade customers to pay earlier in return for some favour, special offer or discount?

c) Can you negotiate longer payment terms, even on a temporary basis with your suppliers?

d) Can you negotiate an overdraft limit with your bank? This will be easy if you've kept your bank manager well briefed over the previous months and if you can show them a well planned cash flow.

e) Can you raise any further equity investment from your investors (including yourself)?

f) What costs can you cut, even if only temporarily? Every penny counts.

g) What orders to your suppliers can you delay?

Work through this checklist and put as many of these into action as you can. Make your staff aware that saving money is important – openness is the best policy. Get your accountant or your bookkeeper to give you advice on the situation. You need to be sure that this is a short term blip rather than a long term trend. Above all, don't give up. It may seem scary, but you will get through it and nobody will die (unless your suppliers have mafia connections).

3. I can't find a good person to recruit for a key position.

One of the biggest challenges facing small businesses is finding the right staff, at the right price. Big companies just seem to throw money at people in management positions, and entrepreneurs in the growth stages of their businesses just can't compete. But a common mistake made by big and small companies alike is to try to recruit on qualifications and experience. What really matters in the entrepreneurial environment is attitude, a couple of key generic skills and a willingness to learn. If someone has the right work ethic, the right communication skills, the right people skills and is willing to learn any of the specialist knowledge they may need, then they are the perfect candidate for you.

So start looking around your existing team. Who has the right attitude? Who is good with people? Who is keen to learn? Is it the right time to see if they would like a challenge? Otherwise, change your recruitment process so that you are looking for these qualities more than anything else. Look for people with this potential and you'll be amazed what they can achieve.

4. I'm so overworked and stressed.

This often stems from point 3 above, but also from an unwillingness to delegate. Try an experiment: take a day off work and sit in the garden with a beer and a book all day. Go back the next day and see if your business has collapsed. No? Okay, take a week off. Is it still there? Take a fortnight off. Once you've proved to yourself that you're not as essential as you thought you were, start to relax a bit more and take some more days off here and there. You should also start to worry less about every detail when you are at work – let other people sort it out. Your job is to set the overall direction of the business, find the right people to take it there and then get out of the way while they get on with it.

5. A big competitor has started a price war.

This is a war you can't win by fighting it on their terms. The first thing you should do in this instance is to look for ways to specialize and to add service to what you do. These are battles they don't know how to fight and they mean you'll eventually win the war. Head for niche markets where people will pay more to get something that is tailored exactly to their needs, is higher quality or comes with a much better level of service.

6. I'll never be able to retire or sell up – who would take over?

This takes us back to point 3 again, and the overall problem that most businesses don't have a good succession plan in place. What would happen if you fell under a bus tomorrow? Who is your natural successor? You need to be developing people and grooming

147

them to follow in your footsteps. This involves training, but it also means involving them more in the day to day running of the business at the moment so they know how everything works.

CRISIS PLANNING

Life doesn't always go smoothly, and your business could be faced with challenges. Although they are highly unlikely, such challenges are worth planning for because they could cripple your business if they happen and you have no plan.

Buildings do get damaged by fire or flood. They may be broken into. Team members may be involved in accidents on the premises, in their cars or elsewhere. Your IT systems may crash (and it might be pushing it to call this one unlikely!).

What would you do if any of these happened? Would your business survive? Most companies don't have a plan, and nearly all companies who are affected by one of the above go out of business within two years of such an event, as a direct result of it happening.

It may seem depressing but it really is worth spending some time on planning for these eventualities. You don't need to plan for every possible event though – you can categorize them under a few key events, such as:

1. Temporary loss of or damage to premises.

This could include fire, flood or burglary. It's anything that means you can't access your premises for a few days, or there is some damage which means your premises aren't fully available. Will you send non-essential staff home while the incident is dealt with? Who is essential in different scenarios? Could you have a reciprocal arrangement with another local company under which you could use a few spare desks in their offices for a couple of days in case of emergency?

2. Permanent loss of premises.

This could include the same as above, but on a more serious level. It's anything that means you completely lose the building and everything in it. You need to plan for finding new premises, how the company will work in the meantime, what the fallback plans will be for continuing your services to customers, and how you will communicate with your team, your customers and your suppliers. You will need to plan for immediate but short term temporary facilities, as well as how the problem will be solved on a more permanent basis.

3. Loss of information systems.

This could be a separate incident, or could be as a result of the points above. It might involve computer systems or paper files. Either way, what plans do you need to put in place for backing up your information (and having backups offsite. It's no use having lots of backups that also get destroyed in a fire!)? How will you replace your IT equipment quickly? Who will oversee this?

4. Injury accident involving team member(s).

If this is an in-work accident you will need to have plans to get someone to hospital or to call an ambulance. You may need to have some members of the team trained in first aid. You will need to record the accident in your accident book and you may need to report the accident to the Health and Safety Executive.

5. Fatal accident involving team member(s).

This is your worst nightmare, and thankfully it is highly unlikely, but it does happen. In the UK, 220 people died in workplace accidents last year and many more died on the roads.

You may have other possible emergency scenarios on your mind, depending on your industry. In each scenario, establish who will be in charge, including an ordered list of who will take over if the person above them on the list is not available. You have to have someone who is clearly in charge in an emergency situation.

In the rest of the plan for each incident, work out what action is needed what communication is needed, and so on.

Now you have scenarios for different incidents, and plans for what you will do when they happen, you can also put into place preventative measures and systems to help things run more smoothly.

First, prepare an Emergency Plan folder. This should include:

1. Copies of the plans for each scenario above.

2. Contact details for your insurance company and any policy details.

3. Contact details for local emergency services.

4. Contact details (home and mobile) for every member of staff.

5. Contact details for local service providers, such as vehicle rental, office rental, office furniture sales, IT systems and telephone providers.

Every one of your managers should have a copy of this folder at home in a secure place, and you should have a couple of copies stored securely in the office.

Second, examine whether you could be taking any further preventative action, or actions that will minimize the impact of an incident. This could include insurance, installing more fire extinguishers, or improving safety training.

SELLING YOUR BUSINESS

Some entrepreneurs see their business as their life's work – something they never want to give up because it is their dream, their baby. Others see their business as an asset that they will one day want to realize by selling.

This will certainly be on the agenda if you accept investment into your company from business angels or venture capitalists.

Some of the exit routes you could consider include:

1. Selling to your management team.

If you've put enough focus into finding and developing the right people for your management team, they will be a smart group of people, and it's often the case that they would like to have a go at running and owning the company they have been part of building. This is called a Management Buy-Out, or MBO, and is very common.

2. Selling to an outside entrepreneur.

There are entrepreneurs who have sold their company, or business people who have just left a high-powered job, who would like to own a business but not have to go through the difficult start-up phase. This is called a Buy-In. There are combinations of this with the first option above, where an outside entrepreneur combines with your existing management team in what is called a BIMBO. I'm not kidding.

3. Selling to another company.

This is perhaps the most common exit route for entrepreneurs. Imagine you have spent ten years building your new solar power company from nothing, then Shell decide they want to get into that business quickly so they offer you a cool £50m for your company. This is how entrepreneurs become seriously rich.

4. Floating your company.

This is the least common exit route, simply because it's costly and time consuming. You can choose to list your company via an Initial Public Offering (IPO) on Ofex, Alternative Investment Market (AIM) or the main market. This means that you offer shares for sale to the public and financial institutions and then your shares are traded on the exchange. However, this is generally just an exit for your investors, as you are likely to be locked in for a period of two to five years after flotation in order to keep the new shareholders happy.

If you know that you will want, or need, an exit route in the next two to five years it is worth starting to work towards it now. All of these routes will take a minimum of six months, but are more likely to take a year or two to bring to reality.

But you can start researching companies who might like to buy you in a few years' time, keeping your eye on key competitors, possible new entrants to the market and so on. You can also work on grooming your management team to be keen and able to take over from you – as, regardless of the exit route you choose, that is the only way you will ever truly be able to leave the business, if you know it is in safe hands.

CELEBRATING SUCCESS

Having reached this point in the book you'll know that there's a lot of hard work involved in having a successful business.

When you have any success in your business it's therefore worth a celebration. This can take whatever form you like – cakes, beers, champagne, a night out, a weekend outing or anything else that you and your team would enjoy.

Celebrating success is an important part of your job as the leader of the company – and it's one of the best bits, so go on, go a little wild!

5

Entrepreneur case studies

My aim with the *Small Business Handbook* has been to help you get to grips with all the 'detail stuff' that most entrepreneurs struggle with. If you can make this side of your business run smoothly it will free up your time to focus on the more creative elements, and making sales!

We've looked at the regulations you need to comply with, best practice that can help you run a better business, and advice that will help you avoid pitfalls.

But we mustn't forget that being an entrepreneur isn't a simple checklist. You don't become a millionaire simply by ticking off the points to say that you've complied with the regulations and you've also put good systems into your business. If it did then we'd all be hearing about Malcolm Jones the accountant in the media instead of Richard Branson the entrepreneur.

Being a successful entrepreneur requires a few other magic ingredients that it's hard to put your finger on because each person who makes it uses a slightly different recipe. This isn't a world of rules where there's only one way to do it it's a case of finding what works for you, your team and your customers.

The best way of learning about these attitudes and skills is by studying the work of other entrepreneurs, and that's the reason for this section of the book. You've got the 'detail stuff' covered now, so let's find out about the magic ingredients to make your business into a soaring success.

INTERVIEWS WITH ENTREPRENEURS

The best way to learn from others is in their own words. So, in this book there are two sets of interviews with sucessful entrepreneurs who have been there and done it. One set of interviews follows this section, in print. The other set are on the CD-Rom in the back of the book, in audio form.

The great thing about being able to listen to interviews is that you're hearing the entrepreneur in their own words. You can hear what they were really excited about and what they were really nervous about. I hope you enjoy them.

INTERVIEWS ON THE CD

On the CD in the back of this book you can hear first hand accounts of how the following people started their business, and what they've learned since:

- Sahar Hashemi started Coffee Republic with her brother, and then floated it on the London Stock Exchange before leaving to pursue a writing and speaking career. As this book goes to press she's now working on a new startup making fat-free sweets!

- Richard Reed is one of the co-founders of Innocent Drinks, a fast-growing company that has achieved an incredible amount in a very short space of time, and now dominates the UK market for fruit smoothie drinks.

- Liz Jackson is the founder of Great Guns Marketing, a telesales company. She's still only in her 20s but has a number of awards already for her success in starting a business from her living room and turning it into a multi-million pound company.

- Simon Woodroffe is now known to millions for his role as an investor in BBC TV's Dragons' Den programme. As an entrepreneur his claim to fame is starting Yo! Sushi, and he is now working to expand the Yo! brand into other areas.

You can listen to the interviews by putting the CD into your normal music CD player – or you can put it into your computer's CD-Rom drive to access the sample documents.

Further reading

If you want to delve deeper into the stories here in print or audio, four of the people featured have their own books:

Sahar Hashemi co-authored *Anyone Can Do It* which is published by Capstone Wiley.

Liz Jackson's book is simply called *Start Up!* and is published by Prentice Hall Business.

Simon Woodroffe's book is called *The Little Book of Yo!* and is published by Capstone Wiley.

John Barnes' book is called *Marketing Judo* and shows how to build a business using brains not budget. It's published by Prentice Hall Business.

Reading or listening to entrepreneur's stories is one of the best ways of learning to make your own business a success, so I recommend buying as many entrepreneur biographies as you can, listening to interviews, reading magazines, etc. in order to soak up their experience and expertise.

INTERVIEWS TO READ

In this section you'll find interviews with four other highly successful entrepreneurs, with real life lessons to add to the ideas, advice and regulations that we've covered so far in this book.
These aren't superheroes, just people like you and me, who worked very, very hard to achieve their dreams. I hope you find their stories inspiring as well as informative.

These interviews were originally recorded for publication on Red Business, which is a regular audio programme for entrepreneurs. Thanks go to the producer of Red Business, Pam Reed, for setting up these interviews and editing them (I'd often record nearly two hours worth!) to bring out the key points. You can find out more about Red Business at **www.redbusiness.biz.**

Paul Theakston

Founder: Black Sheep Brewery

In ten years the Black Sheep brewery has established itself in the premier league of independent brewing. In this time it has earned a solid reputation for good beer – with product quality being the best foundation for a lasting business. However its most successful achievement in the business sense must be the creation of the Black Sheep brand.

It's something that independent brewers struggle to achieve over the promotional noise created by the big internationals, who can afford to throw millions at advertising campaigns, PR, special offers and sports sponsorship.

Black Sheep has built a brand that undoubtedly creates loyalty among its customers. It has achieved this through a customer magazine, promotions with landlords and visits to its brewery which all have the effect of emphasizing the love of real ale and a sense of fun suitable for serious drinkers. You may have seen for yourself the 'Baaaa Menus' in pubs that serve Black Sheep.

This brand has largely been created by accident because it's the natural style of the founder of the brewery, Paul Theakston.

He was educated at the public school, Sedbergh – which he says certainly lived up to its motto 'The stern nurse of man'. He has memories of cold, wet and muddy cross-country runs across the fells, and on leaving the school he swore he would never run for recreation again.

He didn't achieve great academic success and his school report when he left described him as 'lackadaisical'. His careers master had suggested he take a degree in social studies, but when Paul attended an interview at Nottingham University he didn't even know what social studies was and didn't get a place. Instead, he went travelling in Norway for a few months before returning to join the family firm – Theakston's Brewery in Masham, North Yorkshire – at the bottom of the ladder.

After working there for a short while he went to do a year's training at Mansfield brewery before returning to Theakston's to become a brewer. Three years later everything changed in the family firm.

My father died in 1968. He was only 45 – he got leukaemia and died quite unexpectedly and in very short order. It was at a time when a lot of small breweries were folding up or being taken over by large breweries. My uncle only saw the demise of the small brewery, but I saw the potential that lay in small breweries and a good product and that there was an opportunity to go forward and make the business bigger.

It was at this time that the Campaign for Real Ale (Camra) was beginning to take off in reaction to the growth of mass-produced beer and lager. Camra was campaigning for people to support smaller breweries and buy cask beer – just the sort of boost that Theakston's needed. It was this swelling of support for real ale that led Paul Theakston to believe that the family brewery had a future – but he seemed to stand alone in this belief. This led to the first of a series of family battles and fallouts. In the end Paul's uncle decided to retire and the younger generation took over at the end of 1969.

Paul Theakston became Managing Director at the tender age of 23 without any training and was supported by his cousins who became non-executive directors.

The market was quite interesting, there were things to do, and there was a changing scene. The brewing industry is always changing. We complain today that it's changing, but brewers have been in a changing market since probably the 14th century.

Despite these challenges the new management succeeded in growing the brewery progressively until they were doing 250–300 barrels a week. This was essentially the capacity of the brewery, meaning that further growth would require substantial further investment.

Just as the company was planning to make this investment another opportunity arose, but what seemed like a great opportunity would lead to the company losing its independence.

Suddenly, and it was suddenly, we had the opportunity as a business to buy what was the old state management scheme brewery in Carlisle. Somebody rang us up and said they had an option to buy it, they didn't want it but would we like it? We went to look at it, and it was 80 miles away, at least 10 times the size of Masham, and with all sorts of bolt on goodies – 15 wagons sitting in the yard in a row, a bottling plant, a kegging plant – all sorts of things we didn't have. We'd already begun to talk about lifting Masham's production up to 500 barrels a week – and there for the same money was this brewery sitting like the Mary Celeste, hops in the store, casks waiting to be filled. Being Yorkshire and bargain hunters we couldn't resist it. We went and knocked on the bank manager's door and he said yes, so we bought it. That was quite an adventure. It enabled the company to become something it couldn't have been if it had been restrained by the size of the Masham brewery. But of course it brought some problems with it.

One of these was the amount of money needed to develop the new site and to fulfil the opportunities it presented. The bigger brewery needed far more working capital than was available. As a result the company had to bring in outside shareholders for the first time, both individual business angels and ultimately an investment trust.

The business continued to grow and all appeared to be going well until greed sparked a power battle.

One of the external shareholders decided that he was going to put a scheme together that would have resulted in a majority of the company going to another external individual. This was done without the knowledge of the rest of the board, and presented as a fait accompli at a board meeting – it was quite a shock. The lawyers became involved, questioning whether shares could move from a to b to c to d, and to cut a long story short we ended up in the high court in London with a million and a quarter pounds of legal fees fighting over a three and a half million pound company.

To save the company from getting into the wrong hands Paul looked for a white knight and found one in the shape of Matthew Brown, another large independent brewery.

In the middle of 1984, after having a judgment in our favour, the other side capitulated, and the company went lock, stock and barrel to Matthew Brown as a wholly owned subsidiary.

Did he feel like he had a knife in his back?

Yes, I probably did. It's a long time ago now and there's a lot of water under the bridge. But it wasn't the way to do it.

Matthew Brown was in turn acquired by Scottish and Newcastle, who said they were happy to offer him a management position elsewhere in the company but they wanted their own man to run Theakston's. The alternative was a golden parachute. After ten days thinking it over Paul walked away from his family firm with a pay off.

> *The package was OK, but it wasn't enormous. My wife and I sat at home and wondered what to do. We looked at a number of things but we kept coming back to brewing as it was the only thing I know anything about, and the more I thought about it the more I was keen to see if I could re-establish independent brewing in Masham.*

As luck would have it Paul discovered that there were some suitable buildings in Masham that had just come onto the market. After that the question of money reared its head, as the whole project was developing a life of its own and looked to be larger than he could fund himself.

> *It was one of those moments where you have to decide between a larger part of a smaller cake or vice versa. The yeast was rising strongly in this cake and it was developing into a bigger enterprise than originally conceived. We had to go and hunt money to support it. I was keen that we should be well capitalised at the outset, I didn't want to be lying awake at night wondering what the bank manager would say in the morning.*
>
> *We trawled around some of the venture capitalists with our business plan. They patted us on the head and said 'looks good but you only want a million. Why don't you bolt some pubs onto it and we'll lend you 15–20 million'.*
>
> *In the end we ended up doing a business expansion scheme, which was then in operation as a means to allow private individuals to put money into start up or early stage businesses. We were allowed a maximum investment of ¾ million, and in fact we were oversubscribed by 50% and it really hurt sending cheques back to people! The following year we did another one and raised another ¾m.*

Over the summer of 1992 Theakston stitched his new brewery together, adapting the buildings, moving the vessels in, piping it all together, and starting to build the team.

> *In the middle of September we had the magic moment when we did the first couple of brews. We did a bitter on one day and a special on the*

second day. There was a week of brewing and a day or two for it to settle, then the feverish moment when you open the tap to see what you've produced. The bitter was awful really, so we threw that away – it's the only brew that we've thrown away in the history of the brewery. The special that we did we actually sold to Marks and Spencer's as bottled beer.

From October 1992 we started selling to the trade, where we'd warmed up 75 or 80 accounts. It was an amazing moment when some money actually started flowing back in, rather than just paying out while we were setting it all up.

Black Sheep is now selling more beer than ever – including a fair amount in export markets. The business is well established in its market and the product quality, backed up by the strong brand, means the company looks set for further growth. These days Paul must sit a little more easily in the managing director's chair, but were there ever any doubts?

On a head-in-sand basis I knew it was going to work – it had to work. Thank God it has done in the end. We did have one or two sweaty moments in the early years – one or two earnest conversations with the bank manager despite all the capital behind us, but beyond that it's gone very much as I foresaw it and yeah, it's gone ok.

I'll drink to that.

Simon Murdoch

Founder: bookpages.co.uk (now amazon.co.uk), Screenselect.co.uk, friendsabroad.co.uk and many more.

Simon Murdoch is an internet entrepreneur. His first big success was the on-line bookseller he sold to Amazon, where he then spent some years as UK Chief Executive. Simon's interest in technology started at a young age, and while doing a PhD his entrepreneurial streak emerged when he started doing some freelance programming for a local software company.

So when did he first get the idea of striking out on his own ?

> *It was quite a bit later actually, when I finished the PhD I went to work for this software company Triptic – they are just outside London – and I went there actually as a software manager to manage development projects and really it was probably two or three years after that before I saw my own career as becoming an entrepreneur.*
>
> *This software business was relatively small and in those days, in the mid to late 1980s, the whole software industry was effectively being created – obviously the PC had a massive effect on software as well as on hardware and we were learning as went along how to develop programmes for business. 'We were working on systems for construction companies and for publishers, and eventually by chance really, we got into bookselling systems for stock control. So while working there, and involved initially in developing products, because it was a small company I also got involved in sales, marketing and eventually in accounts as well and so got a very good all round experience of what it is like to run a small business. The company had two or three different cash crises which lots of small software companies did – and still do of course – and that really gave me the opportunity to get involved as an investor and then eventually became the managing director of that company and a majority investor in the business. So I kind of fell into entrepreneurship just by being in the right place at the right time with this software business Triptic.*

So where was the money coming from to enable Simon to invest?

> *This software business had a turnover of between £1 and 1.5 million and when it had a cash crisis it needed £20,000–£50,000 to help tide it over so I typically was putting in between £6,000 and £10,000 and I*

persuaded various other people to co-invest and really fell into the whole process then. I didn't have any money behind me but we effectively built up the business and became a market leader in computer systems for book shops in the UK and we survived those difficult times just by borrowing from other individuals and by extending my credit card.

That's a lot of confidence – to believe that you have the business skills, that you can assess that the business is worth investing in, and that you can then do something to help turn the business round. More than that, to put that sort of money on a credit card, Simon must have had a lot of self-belief. Where did that confidence come from?

Some people might say it's stupidity. I have always actually had a huge amount of belief in myself and I remember when I was at school I would often just have a very strong internal feeling that I was going to be successful. A drive I suppose that I think you need that sort of thing to be able to take the knocks when you are running a business. So I think it is an innate thing in me which has been helped by the fact that I have always been very successful through my academic career – I mean I did very well in A levels, I got to Cambridge, I got a first from Cambridge, got a PhD – all those sorts of things – somehow got external validation from the academic side anyway that helped me to reinforce my self belief.

So when did Simon decide that it was time to move on from Triptic?

Well that's an interesting process. What happened was that I became the Managing Director of Triptic at the end of 1990 – it was still a business in a challenging market, the strategy of the company was selling full systems, turnkey systems for booksellers and developing bespoke software. So for example we developed a big customer ordering system for WH Smiths, we had stock control systems in the Dillons shops and Hammick shops and these sorts of things.

Then what happened was of course the internet came along and we saw that quite early and we talked to a lot of our customers about whether they should be on the web selling books and then obviously Amazon.com launched in the States – that was in 1995 and as I was watching this and over the subsequent year or so I was thinking – we were very keen to get some of our customers to commission us to develop internet book selling operations.

Unfortunately for various reasons, the big guys at Waterstones and Dillons either didn't want to do it or chose to develop their internet services with other people so eventually I just decided that if none of the big guys are going to choose us we will do it ourselves and compete with them. That was the genesis of Book Pages the internet bookselling operation I set up. That was in the middle of '96 that we founded that company and then launched it in about December '96 to sell every book in print in the UK and to anybody in the world over the internet.

At that time, the internet was still in its infancy as far as the wider world was concerned and the dot.com bubble was yet to happen. How did Simon go about raising the funding and getting the backing and the resources that he needed to launch Book Pages?

Yes that was really challenging. There were some people investing in internet ventures in '96 and '97. We launched the Book Pages service really by effectively borrowing money from Triptic and resources from Triptic so the development people in Triptic created the website and the plan was to repay Triptic in due course once Book Pages could afford to.

I then spent the whole of really 1997 trying to raise money from venture capitalists for Book Pages. We decided the best thing to do was to launch the service, get it growing and then simultaneously try and raise finance for it. I went to quite a lot of different venture capital companies at that time trying to raise £1million into Book Pages and I remember receiving one letter which was absolutely remarkable in late '97 and I forget which VC it was – sent me a letter saying 'thanks for your plan but we don't want to invest in your business because we have already invested in an internet venture'.

At that time they thought that investing in one internet company was all they could possibly manage. It was an extremely frustrating experience because we were growing very fast at that time. Eventually through a friend of a friend I found a small group of Angel Investors who did put the £1million into Book Pages in January 1998 and one story I often tell about that time – it was very frustrating in that in December 1997 our bank manager from HSBC came to see us at the end of 1997 and said that they weren't going to allow Triptic to continue having an overdraft facility if we carried on funding Book Pages. Effectively the bank manager told us to close down Book Pages in December 1997.

This was another example of the perseverance really, I thought that was the wrong decision and didn't want to do it so I put the letter in the filing cabinet and ignored it. I was rather lucky because the particular branch manager that had sent this letter then happened to move on at Christmas and we kept within our overdraft limit and the bank never pushed us to close down Book Pages, and in January 1998 we raised £1 million finance – so I am glad I didn't take the bank's advice. But very soon after raising this £1million of finance we ended up selling the business to Amazon.

I remember the money came in in January 1998 and just by coincidence almost immediately we started talking to Amazon.com and they bought Book Pages in April 1998 so there wasn't time really to prove that we could do it on our own to be honest.

And how did that conversation with Amazon start?

What happened was that they simply e-mailed us and then phoned us up to talk about talks and then I met up with Jeff Bezos and one of his colleagues Alan Caplin and we just got on really well. We found that obviously they were hugely bigger than we were by that stage and they had had a lot of finance even by early '98 but we had the same sort of attitudes about doing the best possible jobs for customers, both very keen on minimizing the running costs by having technology used throughout the business as much as possible and just found that we got on really well.

So I think that that sort of chemistry about having similar attitudes to the business and the management style was the key thing that he liked and meant that they were interested in buying Book Pages because that gave them a core team and we had just over 20 people by the time that Amazon bought us to de-risk their launch in the UK.

Simultaneous to talking to us – and I am sure our competitors in the UK – they were also working on a strategy to build from scratch a service in the UK, but they decided – the way he explained it to me – that by buying Book Pages and having a team that already knew the market, what the customers wanted, already knew the supply chain, that was reducing their risk in making it likely and it certainly turned out this way – that they would grow much quicker in the UK than if they had built it themselves.

How did Simon find it to deal with Jeff Bezos?

Two things, he's got huge aspirations – right from the beginning, I am sure you will remember that he talked about Amazon being earth's biggest book store – but he chose books just because it was the right category to do on the internet first and he always had an ambition of being the largest e-retailer in the world and I think that those huge aspirations were incredibly important.

I think that the other thing is that he is extremely smart about business strategy. He came up with some wonderful things to discuss and build the culture of the company. Right from the beginning again he was extremely keen on the idea that the company would eventually be a retailer and therefore would have low margins. Obviously they were a retailer right from the beginning, but the idea of the internet was that you had loads of money and could do things expensively – in spite of that he had the vision to see that when Amazon got to scale, the profitability was going to be dependent on having low cost base and so he drummed it into everybody in the business that we are a frugal company and frugality was a word that you heard very frequently within Amazon.

He had this wonderful thing that every desk in the business had to be made out of a door and this was an icon for how Amazon was frugal. His very first desk when he set up Amazon was a slab of wood which he stuck four wooden legs on and he was very keen that everybody in the business had a door desk. He had several other aspects like that which just really built the culture of the business in a smart way that really matched a good strategy for where Amazon was going to get to. So, huge aspirations and very, very smart about corporate culture and business strategy.

Surely Simon was very attached to the business – was it a hard thing to do? It was Simon's idea, he had started it, it was the first one that was truly his from scratch. Was it like losing your 'baby'?

Obviously there is that down-side that you have less control when you are part of a larger organization but for us it was exactly the right deal to do as well. The main reason being that between July '96 when we set up Book Pages and this time April '98 it became clear that to play in internet commerce you need a lot of cash and we found fund raising so difficult and we knew that the £1 million we had wasn't going to be enough to get us to scale and to become a Europe-wide or global organization.

It made a lot of sense for us to fit within Amazon and it turned out to be very good for all the shareholders of Book Pages because of course the Amazon shares went through the roof after we were bought and we were bought mainly for shares and it was a great learning experience for me and everybody else within Book Pages just to work within an organization with such huge aspirations.

One of the phrases that Jeff Bezos coined, and was frequently heard within the company, was 'work hard, have fun, make history'. And it does sound a bit naff to English ears but actually it was incredibly motivational to be within an organization that everybody in the press was talking about and all round the world people were talking about us in dinner party conversations – we were at the hub of growing a business that was on everybody's lips and you did feel like you were making history. It was really very, very exciting in those early days of '98/'99 being part of Amazon.com.

When did Simon get itchy feet and decide that he had done what he could at Amazon, and that it was time to go off to new ventures?

I am very keen on early stage growing companies where I can make a difference and Amazon started to get to feel like a company where it wasn't really me in control in the way that I wanted it to be. At the same time my partner – one of the angels that had invested in Book Pages – had an opportunity to get into Venture Capital so he and I worked together to do a deal with Chase Capital Partners to become venture capital investors and that's what we did next so in the end of '99 we set up a deal with them where we became their internet investing affiliate company.

We set up a company called Episode 1 Partners. It's role in life with Chase's money was to find internet companies to invest in in the UK and Europe which would have the same sort of meteoric growth as say Book Pages/Amazon could or Lastminute.com.

And does Simon get a buzz from this?

Yes I do. If we talk about some of the businesses, we have Screen Select which is a DVD rental business selling the service for a monthly fee to consumers in the UK to borrow three DVDs on a rolling revolving library. A business like this is great fun to work for and I am doing a lot of time in Screen-Select at the moment because it goes from a blank sheet of paper, we only launched in September last year, to seeing something now where we got literally tens of thousands of DVDs being sent out every week. To be instrumental in setting up a company and helping it be successful in that sort of way is really exciting even though I am one step removed because I am not the boss of the company. But I do find that very fulfilling.

John Barnes

Founder: Harry Ramsden's Fish and Chips, La Tasca Tapas restaurants.

Had it not been for Jack Straw's brother, John Barnes might never have had a business career and Harry Ramsden's might never have become the biggest name in fish and chips.

John was at Manchester University, harbouring a desire to become a politician. These were the days of sit-ins and demonstrations, and John stood for office as president of the students union in 1969, leading the race until being beaten at the last count by Ed Straw, brother to the now UK foreign secretary, Jack.

Nursing his pride he went instead to work for Procter and Gamble who make a point of recruiting from the ranks of student politicians.

It was a shock to the system going from student life to a hard-nosed American company who demanded 24 hours a day 7 days a week out of you. You get all the stuffing knocked out of you. I was put out on the road for six months as a salesman in the north east, but it taught me the basics of branding. I was brand assistant on 'Daz' as my first job – and it's still there selling bucket loads in its new pellet format or whatever they've come up with.

P&G believes in brands and backs them with budgets. They have good products; well researched with a differentiated proposition – and then they back their judgement. They don't expect things to work in 6 or 12 months – they build brands for a lifetime.

His career progressed, and after a stint working in the USA launching a new soap brand called 'Coast', he was headhunted to work for Playtex in Paris where he worked for two years before again being headhunted by Pepsi to be their European marketing manager.

But his rise within Pepsi led to a traumatic event, which prompted him to question his ambitions for corporate success.

I was promoted to be general manager of Pepsi in Canada. My wife Pat, our son Edward who was two and Susie our new baby were staying on the 21st floor of the Inn on the Park hotel in Toronto. I was off travelling and there was a massive fire in the hotel. I came back the next morning not knowing anything about it. Six people were killed but Pat and the kids got out down a stairwell full of smoke. It was a huge traumatic experience for all of us, something that changes you. It's indelibly marked on you.

I had to go and recover our stuff from the room we had been staying in, and there were chalk marks on the stairs where the bodies had been found.

It was certainly life changing for me. I really started to question my corporate career, which until then was up, up, up, achievement, achievement, achievement.

The effect on you is quite extraordinary. Pepsi was very good to us, they paid for a holiday, they gave me my old job back in the UK, but something had changed in me. I suddenly thought 'what am I doing here?' I had a young family and I'd been dragging them round the world with me. I think that's where the link between me and self-interested achievement and corporate promotion was broken. It started my love affair with small companies and doing your own thing.

At this stage John took a job as the UK managing director of Kentucky Fried Chicken, and it was during this time that he realized that there was no national brand for fish and chips. If it could work with American style chicken why wouldn't it work with a national favourite?

He'd seen a fish and chip restaurant called Harry Ramsden's when he was playing football in Leeds as a student, and it had left a lasting impression as a grand restaurant with good food.

Richard Richardson, from KFC's advertising agency, suggested that John and he should buy Harry Ramsden's and turn it into a brand. John loved the idea and set about making it happen.

In my naivety I went off to see the chairman of Associated Fisheries who owned Harry Ramsden's as well as a trawler business and lots of other things. I persuaded him to sell for £3m and, with bank and venture capital funding, we gave up our jobs to come north and work out of Harry's old bedroom. People thought we were crazy.

But why pay all this money to buy one fish and chip shop? Why not start from scratch and spend that £3m on an amazing marketing campaign?

The creation of a brand is so hard – I learned that at Procter and Gamble. If it had been 'John Barnes' fish and chips' it wouldn't have worked. It's as simple as that. Whitbread tried it with Hungry Fisherman. We thought that Harry Ramsden's was an embryo brand. It had all these wonderful associations and history having been going since 1928. It was a better place to start than it would have been to do it from scratch.

Suddenly John was running his own business.

It felt amazing. I mean you've got cash flow problems, banks and venture capitalists on your back but none of the corporate support systems – you're on your own. It was worrying as we'd mortgaged our houses and all the things you do to finance a start-up, but I had a tremendous sense of freedom.

What seemed even more audacious than paying over the odds for a Yorkshire fish and chip shop was the announcement, just a year later, that Harry Ramsden's was to float on the third market (now AIM). The bank that had backed them decided it wanted its money back. The venture capitalists didn't want to put any more money in, leaving John with a financial nightmare.

We were really stretched to come up with a solution. It was our broker who gave us the idea of floating it. We went to the underwriters and said we were floating one fish and chip shop and they said we were mad.

But the offer was two-and-a-half times oversubscribed thanks to strong support from local people – leading to the company starting its PLC life with 4,000 Yorkshire shareholders. It also resulted in a lot of positive publicity. John still maintains that the listing was the cheapest advertising campaign he has ever run.

The big break for the company came as the result of a pioneering deal with United Biscuits, in which Harry Ramsden's Fish and Chips went on sale in supermarkets. UB backed this with a huge advertising campaign and Harry Ramsden's brand awareness went from being in the teens to being over 70%.

With clever, and cheap, marketing tricks like this John and his team built the company into a hugely successful, rapidly growing chain with the top brand for fish and chips in the UK, but after 12 years he decided to sell.

What was happening in our sector was that small restaurant companies were increasingly out of favour. We'd been the darlings of the stock market. Our P/E ratio at one time was 45, it was just ridiculous, and then suddenly you're out of favour for the wrong reasons.

We realized very quickly that Harry Ramsden's needed to get into bigger company hands; it needed a firmer base of funding because the stock market was getting rocky. We exited in November 1999, and if you looked at that sector in the following 12 months it was an extraordinary rate of decline.

John stayed at the company for another year to ensure the handover went smoothly then left the office for the last time at the end of 2000.

I still think you can see the fish and chips coming out of my skin, and I had a suit that you could certainly smell fish and chips on. But the sale was right for the shareholders, right for the staff and right for me. Did I regret it? You bet I did. Did I feel bad about it? I did, and I still miss it, I miss it a lot, but with La Tasca I've got the opportunity to do it again.

La Tasca is John's next venture, a national chain of branded tapas bars. Once again he didn't try to start from scratch, opting to buy an established small chain:

We closed the deal at 2am on the 11 September 2001. The VCs said afterwards that we wouldn't have got the deal away if the events in America had happened the day before.

He's taken the role of Chairman this time, employing management to run the business, and this allows him the time to take on other director-ships including Caffe Nero, Yates's, Zoo Digital Group, Galaxy Radio and Arena Leisure. He's also recently floated La Tasca on AIM, in what has been heralded as a highly successful listing.

So what has he learnt in his business career?

Nothing is impossible. There is always an answer, but people give up too soon. You have to expect the turbulence. Don't expect good weather, it's going to be bad weather. Always have another plan at your fingertips.

But having come through all that I'm just incredibly positive about what you can do. You should never give up.

One thing's for sure though, success hasn't gone to his head. Rather than base himself in the trendy parts of London, he runs his businesses from near Leeds. His wife Pat runs a suitably well-branded alternative therapy centre there, and he has a modest office in one corner of the building.

When I phoned up the centre's switchboard a few weeks after the interview, he answered the phone straight away. The receptionist was on a day off so he'd offered to fill in.

This willingness to get stuck in, deal with the customers and understand every part of the business has made him very popular with his employees over the years.

One member of staff looking back at John's twelve years at Harry Ramsden's after the sale had been announced said: 'You've done everything you said you'd do.'

Now that's an epitaph that most entrepreneurs could dream of.

Peter Wilkinson

Founder: Freeserve, Planet Online, Sports Internet, Digital Television Group and more.

There are many recipes for being a successful entrepreneur but the recipe for entrepreneur a la Peter Wilkinson has been highly successful.

Start with a base of low achievement at school:

> *I certainly wasn't the sharpest tool in the shed, I went to St Peter's school in York and I left there with the grand total of one 'O' level in Ancient History, a very good qualification for business!*

Add a liberal dash of early entrepreneurial flair:

> *I started a chip business at school because the food was so awful – I started frying chips in the evening, and that business went through the roof to the extent that by the age of fifteen I was employing eight people cooking and selling chips all around the school, until of course I was shut down because of the smell of frying all around the house, so I must have had some entrepreneurial spirit even at that age.*

Stir in a lack of enthusiasm for working for other people:

> *I ended up having a go at being a programmer. The problem was that at noon on my first day my mother came in to my bedroom to wake me up and asked whether I knew that I was supposed to be at work. I'd forgotten to go.*
>
> *So I got down there, they stuffed me in the corner with a load of programming manuals, which was a little bit like reading the Chinese Daily Herald, and I went home at night and said I don't like it there I'm not going back.*

Finally, ensure that mother refuses to let the heat off until the age of 26, until the entrepreneurial idea is fully baked.

It was in 1983 Peter saw an opportunity to start up on his own and subsequently founded a company called Storm. The company did well, capitalising on a need for big companies to ensure that all their valuable computer data was properly backed up. This company is still going, and is now part of InTechnology plc.

It may seem simplistic to portray such a successful entrepreneur as following the kind of route portrayed by the media – but until this point it seems Wilkinson followed the stereotype to the letter.

The big opportunity that began to set him apart from the rest came when he was at a Leeds United match, sitting next to multi-millionaire Paul Sykes. He was telling Sykes about his idea to launch an Internet Service Provider for business:

> He was interested in technology, so we used to talk and I bounced the Internet idea off him and it appealed to him. He said he'd like to take an investment in that. To me it was a very simple decision to make because he was going to put a million pounds up and it meant I could have a fling at the internet using someone else's money without jeopardizing any of my other business.

The company, named Planet Online, took off in a big way, but an even bigger deal was about to come his way. Wilkinson met Ajaz Ahmed, an employee at electrical retailer Dixon's

> Ajaz wanted to have internet connectivity on every Packard Bell computer that went out of a Dixon's store but on the old £10 a month scenario. That didn't overly appeal to Dixon's.
>
> In fact we were in one meeting with John Clare, the chief exec of Dixon's and a very strong personality, and he said 'The only thing that would turn me on about this is if it was bloody free.' as a throwaway line. I left that meeting thinking he'd be waiting a long time for that 'cause I couldn't think of any way of doing it – but obviously it lodged in my brain.

Not too long after that meeting Wilkinson stumbled on an article about payments that BT would make to companies whose customers used large volumes of call minutes to local rate numbers on their network – known as 'in-payments'. He realized that internet access could be funded through these per-minute charges.

> As soon as I could do it for free I went straight to Dixon's and that deal went through in next to no time really. So I didn't actually take that concept to Dixons as such, there'd already been a lot of negotiations about normal internet connectivity, and when I went along with the free thing the only thing we had to do was remove Packard Bell from the

transaction – not because we were being awkward, difficult or anything, just because there wasn't enough money in it for three parties. There was barely enough money in it for two parties.

The deal was that Dixon's got so much of the in-payment and Planet Online got the rest. They were very happy because they were going to own the site, the portal. That was all theirs. It all got a little bit complicated because we were negotiating the final bits of the Dixon's deal while we were negotiating the sale of Planet Online to Energis. We were moving from one room full of Energis people through to another room next door full of Freeserve people. It got quite complicated at the time.

Fundamentally we felt the simplest way to deal with the situation was that I ended up taking a royalty on the minutes that Freeserve used on the phone network. We had a formula in the agreement where after two and a half years I could cash out based on what had happened and I took that option some time ago.

Another business Wilkinson took away from the negotiating table when selling Planet Online was Planet Football. He used this to make a number of acquisitions, renamed it as Sports Internet, and sold it to BSkyB.

He then went back to focus on his original company, Storm, which is now called Intechnology plc. He made a number of acquisitions, growing the company very rapidly, and then handed over the reins to allow a new chief executive to come in. However, he has recently had to return to the hot seat because of turbulent times in the IT market.

He also has investments in a wide range of other businesses, and was the founder of the Digital Interactive Television Group, which he built into a very successful company operating interactive games and other services via satellite and cable TV. This recently became the latest on his list of businesses to be started from scratch, but sold for millions of pounds.

Peter Wilkinson has achieved an enormous amount in his career already, and looks set to continue his winning streak. But to get to where he is now he's built a large, skilled and loyal team around him. How does he manage these people?

My management style is that if you pay somebody a lot of money to do a job then leave them to do the job – there's no point in me interfering. I'm very involved in any strategic thinking, strategic implementation, but when it comes to actually physically doing the implementation, I do leave that to other people. I have a very quaint expression where I enjoy building the bikes but get really bogged off if I have to pedal them; so I have people who do the pedalling.

I'm a very open person, and I think that if you have an open management style people will know what's going on, people will know what the dream is, what the goals are and I think if they know what they're supposed to be doing they get on and do it and they're fine. If you're in a situation where you don't know if the company's doing well, if it's not doing well, is my job under threat, can I do this, can I do that . . . they're trying to do a job in a strait-jacket.

I probably start on the phone from 8.30 in the morning when I get in, and I'm still on the phone usually past 9 o'clock in the evening – you get a whole load done in those 13 hours, but communication is the key.

Key skills? Grim, grim determination to succeed; I try to do it in as pleasant a way a possible. I don't lose my rag, I don't shout and scream at people; I try to motivate people to want to do it, rather than force them. I think my skill is spotting an opportunity and actually making it happen. It takes huge amounts of energy and determination, but you've got to do it 'cause if you don't your business is just finished.

As you can see this is a potent recipe that keeps rising and rising – but in true Peter Wilkinson style what you see is what you get. There's no PR puff here – he normally refuses to give any interviews at all, which is why you're unlikely to have seen much about him in the press, despite his success. But it's entrepreneurs like Peter who can be the best role models for the next generation.

6

Sample documents

The CD-Rom that comes free with this book includes a number of sample and template documents, and we'll have a look at a few of those on the following pages.

The CD-Rom also includes two sample legal contracts, courtesy of **www.simply-docs.co.uk**, and a special offer for a discount on their other template agreements and documents.

You'll also find other useful documents available from the website that supports this book: **www.flyingstartups.co.uk**

Having template documents can save you a lot of time in your business, and make sure that things are done in a consistent and reliable way – a small amount of well planned paperwork can save a lot of difficult paperwork later!

CUSTOMER PROFILE

This shows a sample customer profile for a web design company, using the 'Customer Profile – Business Customer' template from the CD-Rom.

The idea of customer profile forms is to picture a particular group of your target customers by imagining a fictitious person or company who would fit into that group.

Then, when you come to make key decisions about product development or sales strategy, you can ask yourself 'How would Fred feel about this?' or 'Would Smiths Technologies buy this?'.

Customer profiles really help you to understand your customers on a deeper level.

It's best to create four or five of these fictional customers. This web design companies profiles might be for:

1. An established company with little technological knowledge who wants to get a website (shown in the example opposite).

2. A start-up company with a low budget who wants to create a basic presence on the web.

3. A high-tech start-up with a reasonable budget and a high-specification for a website.

4. A big company with a local base, large budget, but strict requirements.

5. A department of a local government body.

You can find blank template Customer Profile documents on the CD-Rom

Target Customer Profile	
Name:	David McAlister
Age:	56
Job Title:	Managing Director
Company:	McAlister Paper Products
What the Company Does:	Manufactures high quality stationery items such as notebooks, addressbooks, etc.
Their Target Customers:	Until now their main customers have been the major stationery shops to whom they supply 'own-brand' products. Now they want to branch out and develop their own brand for high-end stationery, selling through smaller, more specialist shops, catalogues etc.
Company Background:	David's father started the company after the war, and built it into a successful venture. David took over ten years ago and has had the challenge of brining the company up to date.
Level of Expertise:	They have little experience of the internet, and have had their fingers burned when they paid a lot of money for a website five years ago which has been difficult to update, and has very few features.
Buying Motivations:	They now need to deal with many more small customers, and need an easy way for them to see the product range, order a sample pack and request a visit from a rep. They also want end-user customers to be able to buy product from the site.
Buying Considerations:	They are focused on getting value for money after their previous bad experience. They want to see that the website will help them to communicate with smaller retailers and end-users. They want to be able to update the site themselves.
Their problems:	The supermarkets and big retails chains have been squeezing them on price, hence forcing the change to target smaller retailers with higher value products.
Their worries about purchase:	That they will be taken for a ride by young whizz-kids spouting techno-babble.
Our likely competitors:	Blue Mango Internet and David's nephew who is 'good with computers'.
Key Decision Makers:	David, his wife (who is also involved in the business), the finance director, and the marketing director.

Notes: This is an example Target Customer Profile prepared by the owner of a Web design company.

INVOICE

A range of information is required to be shown on your invoices, but what is required changes depending on whether you are registered for VAT, and whether your company is incorporated (a Limited company).

The example opposite shows a sample invoice for a company that is incorporated and registered for VAT. The requirements are that:

- The Company Registered Address is shown (in the small print at the bottom if the registered address is different from the main trading address shown on the Invoice, which is not the case in this example).

- The Company Registered Number is shown.

- If any of the Director's names are given, the names of all Directors must be shown.

- The VAT Registration Number must be shown.

- The amount of VAT charged on the invoice must be shown.

You'll find sample templates on the CD-Rom for the following situations:

- Limited company, registered for VAT (shown opposite)

- Limited company, not registered for VAT

- Sole trader, registered for VAT

- Sole trader, not registered for VAT

Sample Company Ltd
8 Fictional Street
Nowhere Town
NO1 ERE

Tel: 01234 567890
email: office@sampleco.co.uk

Lovely Client
42 Creation Street
Nowhere Town
NO1 ER2

INVOICE

Invoice Number: 465   Invoice Date: 28/01/2006

Product Code	Description	Units	Unit Price	Price
XB456	Oojamaflips - large	10	£92/each	£920
--	Installation	2 hours	£40/hr	£80
			SubTotal	£1,00.00
			VAT @ 17.5%	£175.00
			TOTAL	£1,175.00

Payment terms: Strictly 30 days net.

Electronic Payment details:
Bank: BarWest TSBC
Sort Code: 01-02-03
Account no: 12345678

Sample Company Ltd. Registered in England and Wales no. 1234567.
Registered office as above. VAT registration number: 123 4567 89

SPECIAL OFFER

Our oojamaflips are the best in the business, but you can get complete peace of mind by also knowing that our support teams are on 24 callout to help you if you ever encounter a problem. Your purchase of 10 or more oojamaflips entitles you to a 10% discount on our 1 year support contract – saving you £200! Call us now on 01234 567890 to take advantage of this offer.

SAVE £200!   Quote this invoice number as your discount code

TRADE REFERENCE REQUEST

When a new customer has applied to open a trade credit account with you, it's important to actually follow up on the references that they give on the form.

A simple way to do that, and to make it more likely that you will receive a reply, is to use a simple, standard letter that the referee can quickly fill out. They can then post or fax it back to you.

A sample letter is included on the CD-Rom, and shown opposite.

Sample Company Ltd
8 Fictional Street
Nowhere Town
NO1 ERE

Tel: 01234 567890
email: office@sampleco.co.uk

Mr Joe Smith
Clients Client Ltd
3 Madeup Avenue
Nowhere Town
NO1 ER2

Date

Dear Mr Smith,

Reference for Lovely Client Ltd

Lovely Client has applied to open a credit account with us, and has asked us to contact you for a trade reference.

I realise that you're busy, so to make this as easy as possible I've listed the questions below. Please simply fill in the boxes and return this to me in the stamped addressed envelope provided. Thankyou for your help.

Yours sincerely,

Name

How long have they been a client of yours?	
What credit limit have you granted them?	
Do they always pay within the agreed credit terms?	
They have applied for a credit limit of £1,000 with us. Do you consider them to be good and credit-worthy for this amount?	
Please provide any other comments that you feel may help us with our decision.	
Please sign here:	
Date:	

MEETING AGENDA

It's important to ensure that meetings achieve their objective and a vital tool to help you is the agenda.

At it's simplest an agenda is just a list of what you're going to talk about, but I believe that you should also outline who is responsible for each item, what documents need to be circulated and read in advance, the maximum amount of time the item should last, and what the purpose of each item is.

This purpose could simply be to provide information to the attendees, or it may be to reach a decision.

A sample agenda is shown opposite, giving examples of different types of items.

You can find a copy of this sample, as well as a blank template for you to use in your business, on the CD-Rom.

Sample Company Ltd

Meeting Agenda

Date: 21st January 2005
Time: 17:00-18:00
Location: Meeting room A, 8 Fictional Street, Nowhere
To attend: Jenny Smith, Andy Jones, Neil Bloggs

Purpose of the meeting: For the management team to review the progress of the business, identify potential problems and adjust the plans to ensure that the business is on track against the business plan and strategy.

1. **Approve last month's minutes**
   Decision
   Neil
   Minutes attached
   1 minute

2. **Recruitment plans for next year**
   Presentation, then Debate, then Decision
   Jenny
   No advance documents
   25 minutes

3. **Sales Update**
   Report, then Questions
   Andy
   Spreadsheet to be circulated by email in advance of meeting
   15 minutes

4. **Finance**
   Report, then Questions
   Neil
   Last months management accounts attached
   10 minutes

MEETING MINUTES

Once a meeting has been held, that is not the end of the matter. It is then vital to ensure that what was agreed at the meeting is put into action.

Each decision should be recorded, and each action point highlighted with a time set for its completion.

These can then be followed up at future meetings.

A sample set of minutes is shown opposite, showing the minutes that resulted from the meeting for which the agenda was shown on the previous page.

You can find a copy of this example, and a blank template for use in your business, on the CD-Rom.

Sample Company Ltd

Meeting Minutes

Date: 21st January 2005
Time: 17:00-18:00
Location: Meeting room A, 8 Fictional Street, Nowhere
Present: Jenny Smith, Andy Jones, Neil Bloggs

Purpose of the meeting: For the management team to review the progress of the business, identify potential problems and adjust the plans to ensure that the business is on track against the business plan and strategy.

1. **Approve last month's minutes**
   The minutes were approved.

2. **Recruitment plans for next year**
   Jenny presented her plans for recruiting new staff in the next financial year.
   She anticipates that we will need 2 new salespeople, 3 more staff in production, and 1 more member of staff to support Neil in finance.
   She believes that we can get economies of scale by advertising the positions at the same time.
   Jenny plans to advertise the vacancies in the local paper, through the trade magazine, and on our website. She will also invite local recruitment agencies to pitch for the work of finding the right candidates.
   She laid out a timetable for the steps that need to be taken (attached).
   Andy asked about the level of experience that could be expected for the salespeople. There was some discussion and it was decided that it was probably best to seek out relatively inexperienced people and provide training, as long as they could demonstrate the right kind of character and enthusiasm.
   Neil asked Andy what salary and benefits he should budget in for that sort of candidate. Andy is to consider this and provide Neil with this information outside the meeting.

3. **Sales Update**
   Andy presented the latest sales figures which show a rise of 12% on this time last year. He showed a graph for projected sales for the next 12 months based on what sales are in progress now, and this showed that this trend is likely to continue. One area of concern is margin, with reps giving too much discount in order to win sales in time for the end of the

bonus quarter. Andy is going to examine our incentive strategy and come up with ways of motivating people to increase the profitability of sales, rather than focusing simply on the timing. He will report back to next month's meeting.

4. **Finance**
   Neil presented the management accounts. Sales are going well, as outlined by Andy, but cash flow is tight at times. We need to focus on collecting money from customers, as it currently takes around 90 days to be paid by most customers, although we have them on 30 day terms. Neil is going to organise a training course to help the sales people understand the importance of us getting paid on time, and equip them with the techniques to achieve this.
   Jenny is going to reinforce this message by including it in her next MD's newsletter.

The meeting closed.

ACTION POINTS:

Jenny

- To invite local recruitment agencies to pitch for finding suitable candidates for the vacancies. Deadline: 12th February.
- To include a message about getting customers to pay us on time in the next MD's newsletter.

Andy

- To provide Neil with details of the packages that he expects to offer to the new salespeople. Deadline: 7th February.
- To examine incentive strategy with a view to including profitability as a target. Deadline: next management meeting.

Neil

- To organise training for the sales team in managing customer accounts after the sale – ie collecting the money. Deadline 30th March.
- To write up the minutes from this meeting. Deadline 16th February.

Afterword

I hope this book proves useful to you in building your business and taking away some of the headaches that it can involve.

I'm passionate about helping other entrepreneurs to start and grow their businesses, so:

1. It would be great to meet you and hear about your company at the online community I run for readers of my books at **www.flyingstartups.com**. Feel free to post any questions or challenges and you'll get a great response from all the other entrepreneurs on the site.

2. I'd love to hear your comments on this book. Which bits did you like? What did you find helpful? Which bits bored you silly? Your comments will help to shape the next edition. My email address is *steve@flyingstartups.com*.

3. I speak at a few business events in the UK (but not too many as I'm reassuringly expensive!), so please do come and say 'Hi' and ask any questions you have. If you want to find out where I'm speaking, or book me to speak at an event, please visit **www.steveparks.co.uk**.

In the meantime, have a great time building your business – and best of luck.

Steve

Index